PREFACE: WHAT AND WHERE? OUR WEBSITE, OUR RESOURCES, OUR BLOG, AND OUR THOUGHTS

Ideas For Potential Clients, Clients, Friends, Family, Colleagues, Adversaries, Judges, Legislators, Change Leaders; It Is Time For Us To Change The Legal Profession, The Delivery Of Legal Services, And Anything Else In Order To Remain Relevant To The Modern World.

This book is organized into eight sections:

1. The Rules of the Game and the Playing Field;
2. Practical Preparation;
3. Family Law and Court;
4. Contingency Fee Cases and Claims;
5. Mediation, Negotiation, and Settlement;
6.Future of the law, Access to Justice, and Law Office Management;
7.Thoughts of the World, Philosophy, Religion, Politics, and *Stuff,* and;
8.Final Thoughts.

I am happy to start this conversation and hope it grows and grows.

I invite you to visit my firm website, www.hunterlawfirm.net and view my four videos, which are my statements of principle and my approach to the practice of law, and to the large red button that guides you to my blog which is fully searchable. Should you elect to subscribe, you will receive notification of each new post.

If you doubt the content of my website, just read this e-mail I got from the relative of a person who needed help:

"Dear Mr. Hunter:

I just wanted to thank you for all of the helpful information and advice your website has to offer. Recently, I helped someone with a West Virginia divorce/custody case and we won because we followed the advice your site offers about organizational techniques and being prepared. The judge even thanked us for being so well organized, and she was sorry the other party did not take the time or make the effort as well Thank you again for all of your help and advice." (Name omitted.)

Messages like that "make my day."

As we prepare to upload this final version, I note the following articles posted since April 27, 2018 which have not made it to the book, but which represent some of my mature thinking.

April 27, 2018: E-Mail Pitfalls and Opportunities;
May 14, 2018: Collaborative Divorce: I Remain Unconvinced;
May 23, 2018: You Have Your Court Approved Property Settlement Agreement: Now What?
June 11, 2018: Low Tech Solutions for the Tech Savvy Lawyer
June 25, 2018: Tying It All Together: Mediation, Unbundling, Collaboration, and a New Paradigm
September 24, 2018: Tying Together Five Years of Law Office Management and Technology: (My September 2018 WVU College of Law CLE Seminar Outline)
September 25, 2018: A Conundrum for Family Courts: What Tools For What Problems # 1
September 28, 2018: A Conundrum for Family Courts: What Tools For What Problems # 2
October 11, 2018: A Lawyer's Thoughts on Slavery and Racism
October 11, 2018: The War Between Women and Men
October. 17, 2018: Gaps In WV Family Law
October 17, 2018: The Challenges to Modern Religion: Part 1
October 17, 2018: The Challenges to Modern Religion: Part II

CONTENTS

I.
THE RULES OF THE GAME AND THE PLAYING FIELD

1.   1,000,000!

Eye-catching figure, isn't it?

One Sunday evening, with the last 100 laps of the NASCAR race playing in the background, I was prompted to write this article by a question from a Facebook friend who has actually read some of my blog. I encourage anyone who reads it to write with their questions. He asked:

Hey Burt, I believe that I have seen you write on Personal Liability Umbrella policies. Is this something that both (my wife) and I would have individually? Are there any things that I need to look for in the policies? No hurry and thanks in advance for your wisdom. Best to you and Nancy.

This is a terrific question. Let's say you are 50 years old with a business, 20 employees, $100,000.00 in savings, $2,000,000 in retirement benefits, a $400,000 house paid for, and a net worth of $3,000,000.

In that case, a personal umbrella is not an option. You risk everything if you don't. I once represented a couple in similar circumstances, and salvaged a denied underinsured (U.I.M.) umbrella claim that saved both their business and their children's inheritance.

But, what if you are younger, have a net worth under $300,000, a professional or business career, $5000 in savings, a house with $20,000 in equity, $50,000 in an I.R.A., 2-3 cars, and a house full of "stuff."

1

In other words, what if you are like "most people"? I say a personal umbrella is also essential.

I have several articles on this subject. Just go to my blog and search for "underinsured," "coverages," "uninsured" or "umbrella" for more details.

But, if you are just reading this, remember, there are two categories of "personal liability" claims:

A.   Claims against you for mistakes your make (run a stoplight, rear end someone); and,

B.   Claims you have against others for mistakes they make that injure you.

If you negligently cause someone to become a quadriplegic, they have a $2,000,000 to $50,000,000 claim. Your option? Bankruptcy, and the loss of most, if not practically all, of what you have.

If someone puts you in the hospital for two months, to be off work for a year, and $500,000 in medical bills, with a permanent impairment that requires you to go back to college for two years for a new skill and pay for replacement prosthetics for life, what do you do if they have $20,000 in per person liability coverage? In short, you are screwed. They pay the $20,000 and probably do not even need to file for bankruptcy. They have nothing worth suing them for.

So, here are the fundamentals of your personal umbrella:

A.   Never, never, never let your insurance representative forget to have underinsured and uninsured coverage at the same limits of your liability coverage. My clients' insurer tried to deny them "umbrella" coverage because their agent forgot to write it! Thanks to a good lawyer who found a brilliant insurance expert to back him up, the coverage was reinstated, and a big part of it paid!

B.   When you get an umbrella policy, coverage of at least $1,000,000, it adds that limit to:

     i.   Your auto personal injury and property liability coverage;

     ii.   Your homeowners;

     iii.   Your auto's underinsured and uninsured coverages.

C.   When you pay for your umbrella, your carrier makes you upgrade the coverage you already have, so now your liability coverage is higher, and your underinsured and uninsured coverages are probably at least $200,000 per person and $600,000 per incident. This is how they can write the umbrella for so little; (Ask your agent, but I think that mine cost less than $100 per year!)

D.   But, you say, "What about that $20,000,000 claim by the paraplegic? We've all heard about those."

     i.   First, those claims are very rare. Do NOT text while driving! We all can probably tell horror stories!

     ii.   When a plaintiff can settle for $1.5 million, faced with the threat that you will file bankruptcy, they almost always will take it and count their blessings. A good lawyer can distribute and preserve that settlement in a way to maximize the benefit of the injured person.

iii.   So, get a personal umbrella, and if you are the guy with a net worth over $3,000,000, buy a bigger umbrella!

2.   Collegiality, Professionalism, and Burt's Lie Detector!

Recently, I needed some letters of support from friends and colleagues, and I got them. It was an uplifting experience to receive such support, but a few of the letters contained a qualification or two that concerned me. Over the years I have heard the suggestion that I can be overzealous in representing my clients, and, "You always believe your client!" These crept into the letters of support, and were a wake-up call that some of my colleagues still do not understand me.

Allowing for the fact, as George W. Bush once famously said, (or was it Bill Clinton?) **"When I was young and foolish I was young and foolish.,"** it has been decades since either of the criticisms above were valid for me. But some labels, once affixed, stick, and these are two that I have to bear.

I have no way to convey to someone who has not been there, what it is like to handle @ 3000 cases on one subject, or 50,000 + hours in one endeavor. Some people could do this and keep doing the same things over and over without learning new and better ways. That is not me.

Faced with a new challenge, I take it head on. If it's a new subject, I read a book or manual. If a new technology or method comes out, I am likely to try it. I consider it a special

4

challenge to figure out how to do something in a different way from others.

It is not my lot in life to come up with a new cure for cancer, to discover calculus, become rich and famous, or found a new religious movement, but that does not mean I want only to take up space in my journey through life.

My job is to complete tasks and solve problems, my family's, my friends', my clients' and my own. Each one is a puzzle to be solved. In my professional life, I MUST gather accurate facts, so being a cheerleader for the client makes no sense. And, I must be an advocate for the best interests of their children and guide them away from hurtful behavior.

And, how do I convince other lawyers that I have an unusual ability to figure out who is telling the truth? They are smart people, and they think THEY have that special skill.

First, I suggest that after you read this, you go to my blog article, May 5, 2010, "*Something Constructive; How to Organize the Facts in Your Case.*" Read it and watch the video. They describe my method, in every case, taken from the LexisNexis CaseSoft suite of software products, to investigate and organize the facts of the case. I first help my client identify the documents, people, and things that populate their particular case. I need to know each such person, address, phone, relationship to the parties, and what they know.

I need the photos, the Facebook postings, text messages, tax returns, deeds, titles, account balances, medical bills, medical records, and the other evidence that will be presented at trial (even though with this stuff, we usually avoid the need for a trial.)

I then need lists, LOTS of lists, of my clients concerns, of complaints against the other party, of facts in my client's favor, or problems they want to solve. FINALLY, after I make them collect these building blocks, we work on the structure itself. They can write or tell me a detailed chronology, and I can put our allegations into something called a pleading, a complaint, a petition, or a motion. When the client cannot provide these things in sufficient numbers, or of sufficient quality, I already have part of my "lie detector" in operation.

I recall the very nasty fellow who claimed to have been the primary care provider of his children who prepared no meals for them, had no cancelled checks to Kroger's, no box of recipes, no favorite meals he liked to prepare. His position, "We eat lots of fast food!" Some care provider! He and I parted ways not long after that, and Burt's lie detector worked perfectly.

I sometimes use imaginary lie detectors or drug tests to get to the truth. I had a client charged with raping his 70-year-old landlady. Not a pretty picture, but neither was the case of my client charged with committing the same act with his 85-year-old grandmother.

I explained to the first fellow that it would be good for me to be able to present to the prosecutor a clear lie detector result but warned him that if he were lying to me, he would fail the test. He was not a mental giant. He gave me a sly look and said, "I beat one in Clarksburg!" 'Nuff said. I had the results of my test. We worked out a plea agreement.

That raises the interesting question of whether criminal defense lawyers even want the truth from their clients? When I finally realized the answer is often "no," I worked to stop doing criminal defense.

And, of course, when I ask my client if he/she is a drug user, and I see wide-eyed innocence in the denial, I simply say, "Great, please go down to the Day Report Center to get us a clean drug screen," or as the Judge says, "Go piddle." The look in the client's eye tells me what I need to know. And, for the ones who are confident they can pass, sometimes I just wanted to know for my own information, but other times, I go ahead and send them, and attach the clean report to the pleadings, or bring it with me to the first hearing as a trump card.

Because they are not making it up as they go along, their stories have a rhythm. People lie all the time, but most like to tie their tale to some core truths. Little qualifications or hesitancies speak volumes to someone who has done 10,000 - 20,000 interviews.

Lawyers need to learn how to read my written replies to their letters of concern or complaint. I may say, "Mr. Jones adamantly denies using the F-word against and flipping the bird against Ms. Jones last week-end, but I have stressed to him the need for courtesy and respect. He has promised me there will be no such behavior in the future.

This paragraph can be interpreted, "I realize my client may have acted like an idiot, but he is not going to admit it. I raised a lot of Cain with him, made sure he understands that no court will consider this behavior consistent with the best interests of the children, and if proven, can cost him some of his parenting rights."

The receiving lawyer simply needs to consider the context of my writing and give me the benefit of not being as stupid as he or she assumes I am.

As for being overzealous, filing pleadings on time, following up discovery with reminders of overdue responses, refusing to accept an answer that no witnesses have been identified six months into the case, complaining when transfer times for the children or child support payments are late, may be zealous, but they are not <u>over</u>zealous.

Accepting client's e-mails at all hours and forwarding their concerns and responses are zealous, not overzealous.

Filing a pleading knowing it is false, piling on discovery just to wear the other party out, calling names such as liar or thief, giving false or incomplete offers of proof (proffers) to the court, and filing frivolous motions are overzealous.

Taking on the persona of your abusive client? That's overzealous. Walking around the other parties' residence without advance notice to her counsel, communicating directly with a represented party, or sending your client to the other party with a settlement proposal to get around the other counsel? NOW, THAT'S OVERZEALOUS!

And all of these things have happened to me and my clients. I do not engage in such behavior. Never have, never will, period.

So, call me opinionated, occasionally tactless, bull-headed, and vain. I have been guilty of all of these. Do not call me a liar. Expect me to keep my word and require my clients to keep theirs. If my client repudiates an agreement made in good faith, without good reason, I will probably withdraw from representing him or her.

And, please use your own skills to gather accurate facts, probe your client's complaint, do not fire off unsupported accusations, and measure your words. Finally, I know the rules for professional behavior and follow them, and I have my own strict standards and follow them too. If you give me the benefit of the doubt, I shall accord the same to you.

3.   Your Legal Checkup and Review; "An Ounce of Prevention"

We are used to the idea of an annual medical examination or "check-up," but not so much for our "legal health." As a young US Air Force JAG attorney, I learned of a concept called *preventive law*. Remember the truth in the phrases "an ounce of prevention" and "a pound of cure." I am happy to offer you that ounce of prevention.

There are firms that focus on complex estate planning for "seven figure" estates. We will be happy to work with you in finding such a firm, but a "legal checkup" is much broader than that. Even smaller estates need a review, updates of your wills, and so much more. And there are other aspects of your legal lives. Here are some of many things we will review or update for a small fixed fee, $500.

A.   **Durable General Power of Attorney:** Most people should have someone they trust explicitly who can sign for a package, open an account, or pay a bill if they cannot. This can be helpful if you are out of the country, but it could be critical if you are in an accident or become medically incompetent. If properly recorded, a "Durable General Power of Attorney" can be used to sign a deed or promissory note AFTER you become incapacitated. That's what makes it "durable."

B.   **Special Power of Attorney:** Special POA's are designed for a particular purpose. In the military, we often prepared special POA's so that a spouse could sign all documents relative to the transportation of household goods. A special power of attorney can be defined as narrowly as you choose, to take your child to the doctor or to sign for a package. At our office, if we expect a check in the mail while on vacation, we sometimes sign a special power of attorney so our staff can deposit it. Special Powers of Attorney are simple, and of course cheap, but they still must be done right.

C.   **Medical Power of Attorney:** As long as you are clear of mind, your "Medical Power of Attorney" is of no force. But, like "durable general powers of attorney," they become critical when you can no longer make decisions yourself. You and the person you pick for your "medical power of attorney" need to have a heart to heart talk. That person needs to know you, where you are in your life, your values, and your tolerances. I have held that solemn position of trust for both of my parents. It is an important decision. Don't leave it up to WV's "medical surrogacy law." That's akin to refusing to have a will and letting the State divide your estate for you (intestacy law).

D.   **Living Will:** I do not like living wills. I think they come from the same source as the "opioid crisis," the profit motive of the medical industry. If you have a "Medical Power of Attorney," why have an "advance directive" controlling those final medical decisions? A cynic might say it is a ploy by the insurance companies to free up medical beds. Why else are they promoted with the fear of "having tubes stuck all over your body"? I say, cover that in your discussion with your Medical surrogate, but we can discuss it. Don't hesitate to do your own reading or get a second opinion.

E. **Your last will and testament:** If you die without a will, you are "intestate." Your "will" will be the one the State wrote for you. You will have died "intestate" and your heirs may be just who you expected, spouse or children, but perhaps not. And, you leave them confused as to the person you wanted to handle the estate. That's the "administrator" or "executor." Many people with simple estates still want to specify "bequests" of personal property, heirlooms, etc., or "real estate" such as Grandma's farm. Don't leave such traps for you family to navigate. They'll be glad you made your wishes clear.

F. If your family is not getting along, and you or someone you love is being pulled to and fro, that's when a lawyer you trust should be consulted. The lawyer will take care to protect his client from undue influence and carry out his un-coerced wishes.

G. And, if you have a blended family or a minor child whose parent is unfit to care for them, or an impaired adult relative, or any of a dozen other challenges? If so, for God Sake, give us a call to discuss it. I have seen four cases in which a person's wishes from the grave impacted who took care of their loved one.

H. Have you reviewed your insurance coverages in detail? Perhaps your insurance agent can do it, but not from the perspective of real world claims, prospects for settlement, and avoiding financial ruin. Why not chat with both of us? I have solid ideas of how much coverage is enough. It is essential for you to carry adequate personal injury and property damage liability coverage.

I. And, uninsured and underinsured motorist coverages when the other driver carries little or no insurance? Just think, the person coming around that curve could put you or your loved one(s) in a hospital for months and pay little or nothing to assist in your recovery. No lost wages, medical expenses, payment for walkers, ramps, care providers, rehabilitation, pain and suffering (which could be immense), and permanent injury. Permanent means a life sentence.

J. Even if you have medical insurance, consider a form of coverage called "medical payments" or "med pay." It can pay $5000-$25,000 regardless of who was at fault and is not a charge against your medical insurance lifetime limit. It can cover deductibles and limitations from your primary coverage, and you can avoid the delay of waiting for the liability carrier to settle with you. Remember, they will not pay until you have recovered and are ready to sign a release.

K. Finally, if you own your home, perhaps a business, have retirement funds, or investments, you will need an umbrella! That is exactly what it sounds like, coverage over and beyond your other coverages, homeowners, auto, under and uninsurable, and liability. Usually it adds at least $1,000,000.00 in coverage, and it is cheap. See my article: http://hunterlawfirm.net/buy-a-1000000-umbrella/12. .

L. Are you beginning to sense that marriage is going downhill? Anyone who sees a divorce or separation as a looming possibility owes themselves and their family to do their homework. Fault, parenting rights, custody, visitation, decision making, property division, debt allocation, alimony, and division of retirement benefits. These are all issues where you can get answers.

M. There are so many other aspects of your legal life. The neighbor who keeps damaging your driveway. The neighbor who seems to think he owns your side of the fence. The relatively minor auto accident that you have been meaning to get settled. The friend who has not paid you back, or that nagging workers compensation claim. Just make your list of concerns and give us a call. We will cover them and more.

II.
PRACTICAL PREPARATION

Each of my new clients receive this instruction sheet. I invite them to discuss any points they may not immediately understand.

1.   Important Instructions to New Client(s); Please Read Carefully and Sign.

Dear New Client:

A.   During his representation, there are certain instructions Mr. Hunter and his staff routinely provide and repeat. The core of these instructions is listed here with the hope you will read them, understand them, and agree to follow the standards of the Court and Mr. Hunter's procedures. Experience shows that your firm commitment to conduct yourself properly and to learn and follow Mr. Hunter's methods will save you money, time, and heartache!

B.   These procedures apply whether your case is a:

    i.   Personal injury;

    ii.   Civil action;

    iii.   Family Court matter; or

    iv.   Mediation.

    (Note: each of these areas has its own set of specialized intake forms.)

14

C.   Please consider anything you post to the Internet to be public. Set your privacy settings to "friends only" but realize any "friend" can share or print, "snag" or take a screenshot of, anything you post, and forward it to anyone they want!

D.   Ponder the previous paragraph while realizing the reverse is also true! Without doing anything illegal or even unethical, you can have your good friends or family keep track of our opponents, or you can review public posts, and your own e-mails, texts, and messages. It is truly remarkable what people post and say. To the extent that it is abusive, profane, offensive, or prurient, it likely will help us demonstrate to a court or jury what the other side is really like. Are they a fit parent? An abuser? Addicted? Dangerous? These "puzzle pieces" help us create the true picture, but they could reveal your less than admirable traits also; be careful!

E.   By accepting Mr. Hunter as your representative, you are agreeing that your Internet posts will conform to reasonable standards of civility and taste, that you will post nothing on pending litigation, that if children are the subject of the litigation, no photographs of or comments about the children will be posted, and that the standard you will follow is that you will post nothing that you would not want your mother, your children, your spouse, your lawyer, or your minister to see. Note: this rule should be flexible and guided by simple good taste and common sense.

F.   Mr. Hunter has a carefully devised method for helping you organize the facts in your case. You are agreeing to follow his methods as best you can, and, most importantly, to ask questions about things you do not understand. Note: especially in cases with lots of facts (puzzle pieces or "objects"), your careful gathering and sorting of those pieces can save you thousands of dollars!

G.   While email is a wonderful form of communication, Mr. Hunter cannot absorb your communications unless you will keep your paragraphs short, 1 to 2 lines, numbered, and to the point!

H.   To the extent you must use more than one email, do so, but recognize that long rambling emails may contain information that is not fully absorbed.

I.   Many Family Court proceedings have very strict rules of disclosure. You will be provided forms for you to summarize "caretaking functions" of your children by you, your child's other parent, and third parties, your property and debt, and other important information. You will be required to prepare complete financial affidavits and to file tax returns and earning information.

J.   AND REMEMBER, Family Court proceedings are confidential so do not talk about them, share them, or post videos or transcripts of the hearings. If others break this rule, let us know!

K.   It will be your responsibility to "do your homework," whether it is a family court matter, civil litigation, or personal injury claim or lawsuit, for example, by getting:

    i.   A duplicate of that credit card bill;

ii.   Bank account information;

iii.   Tax returns with schedules attached;

iv.   Current pay records;

v.   Retirement and insurance documents and policies;

vi.   E-mails, screen shots of text messages, and other digital communication.;

vii.   Digital copies of photographs, and;

viii.   All sorts of other critical information.

L.   I repeat, the fact you do not have an item in your possession at the time it is requested is no excuse. The success of your case will be determined:

i.   By its merits, but also;

ii.   By the diligence and efficiency of your preparation and your communication with your lawyer.

M.   It is critical that you tell your lawyer the truth. By this, Mr. Hunter does not mean simply answering his questions truthfully. If you have:

i.   A felony conviction;

ii.   A domestic violence petition filed against you, whether it resulted in the protective order or not;

iii.	A drunk driving conviction;
iv.	A disgusting Facebook page;
v.	A pre-existing injury;
vi.	A psychological problem;
vii.	A drug or alcohol dependency;
viii.	Or any other fact that you know in your gut Mr. Hunter needs to know,

You must tell him! In other words, Mr. Hunter hates surprises! If there is "an elephant in the room," tell him!

N. By signing this document, you are certifying that you have read and understood each of these instructions and will abide by them.

O. If any of them seem unreasonable, or you do not understand them, please speak with a staff member or with Mr. Hunter before signing.

_____   _____

Client Signature   Date

2. The Nuts and Bolts of Preparing For Your Deposition

First, what is a deposition? A deposition is sworn testimony before a court reporter taken before the trial. It can be an audio recording, or audio and video.

It is part of the discovery process, although a trial deposition can be taken to preserve for trial the testimony of a person who may be unavailable for trial, such as a seriously ill or elderly person, or someone planning to be out of the country.

Depositions are often taken of witnesses to a controversial event such as an auto collision, and they may be taken by a party such as the plaintiff or defendant in a lawsuit.

Depositions are rare in family court cases because of the expense. People paying their lawyer by the hour usually do not want to pay for a deposition, unless it is a key adverse witness such as your spouse's "paramour."

Depositions are the norm in personal injury, medical malpractice, industrial accident, and insurance bad faith cases.

I know one, only one, lawyer who routinely takes depositions in order to run up costs and cow the opposition. I have seen it succeed, and it disgusts me.

Let's assume you are a plaintiff in an auto accident, or the petitioner in a divorce. What do you need to do in order to prepare?

A.   I ask my clients, at the beginning of the case, to read my two articles, in my blog "Perspectives of a Small-Town Lawyer," www.hunterlawfirm.net, "Something Constructive: How to Organize the Facts in Your Case" and "More About Organizing the Facts in Your Case." You can find these articles by entering partial phrases into my blog search engine. "How to Organize" or "More About Organizing" will find them instantly.

B.   **This is where they learn that we collect the "pieces of the puzzle."** We call them "objects;" the people, the documents, the events, the places, and the physical objects that make up their story. This is hard for them, to realize their spouse, spouse's lawyer, children, the other driver, the school bus driver, text messages, e-mails, letters, bills, receipts, building, physical attacks, altercations, and myriad other things are "objects."

C.   **This is because a case is made up of evidence.** A witness's testimony is evidence, but that person may need to produce that phone record, text, photograph, or tax return that confirms the accuracy of the testimony. So, the witness and his lawyer must collect those objects, the pieces of the puzzle.

D.   **The witness must carefully review the pleadings before her deposition.** This is the complaint or petition we filed, or the one served on my client by the other side.

E.   **Also as part of our preparation**, after the objects are identified, and my client's goals and concerns are listed (Burt's "top ten lists"), **we must work off of a detailed timeline**. It is so effective for a witness to know when he and his wife first met, when their children were born, when that domestic violence petition was filed, or when the accident took place, the claim was filed, the doctor's visits took place, and the surgery was performed. We have nifty software that can create a timeline exhibit.

F.   **Witnesses expect the questioning lawyer to be nasty.** Again, I know two lawyers whose persona IS nasty. It is inherent to their personalities. They demean, deride, bully, and insult. It is intimidating and insulting. When pushed to the absolute limit, it is critical for the lawyer, or the adverse lawyer, to seek help from the Court. That happens only rarely.

G.   **More subtle, pleasant, and potentially dangerous is the friendly, professional, conversational, and reasonable lawyer.** They can get you to give in on points the angry lawyer cannot. **And, of course, there are those in the middle, tough, aggressive, but professional and fair.**

H.   The deponent must prepare for all kinds of potential questioners.

I.   After careful preparation, my advice is:

   i.   Listen carefully to the question:

   ii.   If you can answer, do so directly and concisely.

   iii.   If you think the answer makes you look bad, but it is basically as "yes" or "no" kind of question, give the answer! *Do not try to avoid it or give the explanation before the answer. If the other lawyer will not let you explain, your lawyer will.*

   iv.   Do not volunteer facts not requested, become overly friendly, be lulled into a false sense of security *by a friendly questioner or be baited into an argument.*

   v.   When you are done, STOP! *It seems so easy, but it is not. When you are nervous, you tend to ramble. And some of us just like to hear our own voices.*

vi.   If you don't know the answer say so, but do not give up too easily.

vii.   If you know the answer within a range *(It was last winter because there was snow on the ground.)*, then state your range. *It might be "Just over six feet," or "fifty to 100 feet," or "between $35,000 and $50,000." It that's the closest you can get, say so and stop.*

viii.   If you become tired or confused, ask for a break, *water, a restroom, or a snack, and you will usually get it.*

ix.   If your lawyer is objecting or getting angry, do not ignore that! *Something is going on! Be alert. Maybe it's time for you to ask for that break.*

x.   Above all, *tell the truth.*

J.   **My adversaries often say you cannot correct a factual or substantive error**. There may be a technical rule about that that I am not aware of, **but I disagree.** If my client said "Tuesday" and the answer was really "Wednesday," I have them write that in the errata sheet that the court reporter provides.

K.   **I always have my client ask to read and sign the deposition**. It isn't that we mistrust the reporter, but they are human too, and we need to correct those mistakes!

L.   **At the end, I do not care about a paper copy.** *I asked for a digital one so I can index and paste the relevant testimony into software I have for that purpose.*

M.   **Cases can be won or lost in discovery,** *whether by written answers or oral/video testimony.*

N.   **If the deposition is with video, you must make sure your client is presentable,** *although that really is true in any kind of deposition, but remind the witness to a video deposition that the camera will pick up shifty eyes, nervous ticks, and refusals to address the question.*

With these basic rules, and a bit of practice, our clients are well prepared for their depositions.

3.   Digging Down: Short and Sweet

Here's the deal. Whether you have a lawyer or not, you probably will get some forms that are mandatory for your case. Take them seriously. The authors of the forms know you probably won't read the law or rules, so, with luck, the forms can guide you to providing the right information.

For most matters, you will be much better off if I represent you, or you at least pay for a "robust consultation." Right now, they cost $500 and can lead to full representation. You get to decide.

"Mr. Hunter, what tool can I use to gather and organize the facts of my case?"

The Three-Legged Stool

The three essential legs or pillars:

A.   The "Object Lists;" that is the collection of puzzle pieces that make up your case:

i.   People;

ii.   Documents;

iii.   Places;

iv.   Events;

v.   Organization;

vi.   Physical Objects; and,

vii.   "Other stuff," that make the pieces of your puzzle.

B.   Burt's "top ten lists." These aren't the puzzle pieces. Each list has a title, "Things I want to tell Mr. Hunter," "Questions I want to Ask Mr. Hunter," "Goals for Mediation," or "Grievances I have about the other party."

C.   Each time you have a question or idea pop in your head, start a "top ten list" and give it a pithy title. I think of these lists as "memory ticklers." They are essential, but the "objects" are the puzzle pieces.

D.   The Timeline, or chronology: The other two legs, Object lists and Top 10 Lists, provide what you need to create a concise, complete, timeline. Give your lawyer a good timeline, and he/she can tell the judge or jury your story.

Our "Organizing Kit" accordion folder, preprinted fill in the blank forms, and timeline template is what you need to bring to your lawyer, or his staff, the essential material they need to represent you properly.

4. On Organizing and Preparing For Your Case

First, I provide here a link to the PDF version of this article, complete with fill in the blank forms: http://hunterlawfirm.net/wpcontent/uploads/2016/12/hun terlawfirm-get-organized-forms.pdf

This is not theoretical. It is how I begin a case, size up a client and my adversary, gather facts, organize, prepare, and resolve. If I were a "writing roofer," I would tell you how I get that roof to be attractive, durable, and shelter from the elements. This is the same thing. "This Old Lawyer" instead of "The Old House."

My plan is to explain this method in detail, to provide some ideas for conducting a "new client interview" and "follow up interview," to provide insights into how I approach mediation, and to provide some insights into how I use the organized information for a trial or contested hearing.

My method uses some basic forms so the client can save money by collecting the puzzle pieces himself or herself. I have attached my fill-in-the-blank forms at the end of this article.

THE BASIC CONCEPT

(Object Lists, Top Ten Lists, and The Timeline)

Mankind is a story-telling species. We love to share stories. Most of us are not trained in the law or the presentation of evidence, so it does not come naturally to gather it and provide it to your lawyer.

And some of us are not very good storytellers. We ramble, digress, and lose focus. My job as a lawyer is to channel the energy and turn it into something understandable to the court or jury.

In preparing for a contested trial, hearing, or even a mediation, we need a method to gather facts and a plan to organize and prove them. And, as questions and concerns pop into our heads, we must have a method for recording and cataloguing them. That's where "Burt's Top Ten Lists," further below, come in handy.

THE INITIAL INTERVIEW

When I first meet the client, she/he wants to give me a narrative (the story), and sometimes he/she becomes a bit impatient, or offended, if I don't let them tell it.

I ask them to trust that I have learned some things in 40+ years. I explain that I must ask essential questions before it even becomes relevant for me to learn "the story." This allows me to absorb "the story" in digestible bites.

Occasionally, the client turns it into a power struggle. Very occasionally the client makes me realize I do not want to represent that person. So be it. Better to part then than later.

Another indicator is whether a potential client has bothered to fill in our intake forms. Once I confirm they are of normal intelligence and literate, I carefully explain that working with their lawyer is just that, WORK.

It is the client's life, and I need to know she/he is ready to help me gather the facts and do the job to protect them and their family. Some people simply are not willing to make the commitment in their own case. Others are simply unable to, and they deserve our concerted attention too. I prefer the client who is ready to become a willing partner in the endeavor.

MY METHOD

The "three-legged stool" of organizing your case has these components: (Please memorize!)

A.   Object lists:

B.   Burt's "Top Ten Lists," and

C.   A timeline.

Simple, right? Not at all, but if you take it a step at a time, it is manageable. Note: Since writing this I have "bit the bullet" and purchased two subscriptions to the CaseMap Suite of organizing tools, owned by Lexis/Nexis.

OBJECTS, AKA PUZZLE PIECES

Here is the simple part. Objects are the pieces of the puzzle that is your case. Gather and sort them, and the picture appears. Objects are the people; documents (paper and digital); photographs: places; events; physical objects (the knife or brick); and, every other "thing" that will be included in a detailed narrative of the parties and their dispute.

Objects can be the people who know the facts, the potential witnesses. Other puzzle pieces are the personal property (moveable items) and real property (land, houses, and commercial property, the debts, the parties' income, the retirement benefits, the credit card debt, medical bills, debts on property, and the pre- and post- separation budgets of the parties. All those pieces must be present for the Court to "picture" the case.

In a personal injury claim there are witnesses to the collision, an investigating officer, emergency personnel, photographs, the accident report, cell phone records, medical bills, medical records, journals, lay witnesses who know my client well, expert witnesses, and myriad other "puzzle pieces."

In a real estate dispute there are deeds, wills, deeds of trust, angry neighbors (or siblings!), aerial photographs (now usually Google Maps),...you get the point. Every case involves important information, in more pieces than you think.

"BURT'S TOP TEN LISTS"

Top Ten Lists can be more, or less, than ten, but each list pertains to one category. They are my clients' questions, worries, goals, complaints about the other party, and wishes. They are the memory ticklers, the checklist.

The mediators who work with me sometimes ask, "May I see your list?" because they know my client and I will show up at mediation armed with our lists, so we can check them off and not leave mediation without addressing every important issue.

Some clients never run out of questions. I answer them, but I also say, "Be sure to put that down on one of your top ten lists." These "memory ticklers" are the checklists which help drive our preparation. They and the "puzzle pieces" merge to tell the story and complete the timeline. Remember, "object lists" are different from "top ten lists." They are the people, documents, e-mails, texts, physical items, places, events, and organizations that populate the facts of every case.

TWO RULES FOR MY "TOP TEN LISTS:"

Put a title on the top of each list! e.g., "Why is he a terrible parent?" or, "What do I want from this mediation?" or, "What she did to abuse our children?" or, "The reasons I did not cause the collision," or, "My symptoms from the collision," or "My Injuries." Each item must be concise, 1-2 lines, and numbered in a list, directly below the title.

THE TIMELINE

We use the "Object Lists" and "The Top Ten Lists" when we create our timeline of facts. We sort them chronologically. Then we put the important ones into a time line with individual flags.

Some of our timeline exhibits are very long. In those cases, I insist on a second timeline exhibit selecting only the most important items. "Mapping events" in the order they happened is an invaluable tool. Do not go to trial if you have not mapped your events. If you do you will stumble and perhaps fall. Time and sequence are keys!

Timeline exhibits are the "maps" of our presentation. They are the story that we present to the judge, jury, or mediator. Do not forget that instead of a rambling story, our timeline is supported by the witnesses and exhibits we need.

THE INTERVIEW II

There is a fair, but incorrect, criticism of me that I am not a good listener. Being assertive, and anxious to educate, I tend to move the witness along and even to "over-talk."

How do I combat that flaw? That's the whole point of my method! I use my brain to work around my flaws, to the benefits of my clients. I learn what I need from the interview, and we build the puzzle into a complete picture.

And, I only appear to be a bad listener. I ask lots of narrowly focused questions, so I can get to the essence of the dispute.

It is hard for my clients, and even opponents, to envision how tens of thousands of hours of experience allow me to learn much from focused, relatively short, answers. I can filter and understand in a way that I never could as a younger man. And, if it is a "yes or no question," I insist the client answer before explaining. Now that can be tough! I have to chuckle when some guy whose philandering, drug using, wife is wrapping him around her finger, says, "You don't understand!" They think they are the only guy who has ever been through this, but I have known dozens/hundreds of them!

SIZING UP MY CLIENT

I can tell from how a client answers how good a witness he or she will likely be, and we adjust accordingly.

I can turn an average witness into a good one and a bad one into an average one.

If someone breaks down in front of me, I warn them that our opponent's counsel might "make mincemeat" of them if they do not learn to stand up for themselves. If the client gets angry, I point out that if they overreact to someone on their own side, they're going to have difficulty dealing with a determined adversary.

If I ask a "yes or no question" but get an "explanation" in reply, I know they are embarrassed by the answer, so I insist they learn to answer questions directly and explain later.

The Judge will notice in an instant the witness who will not answer a question. And, I must know the worst the other side will have against us, so I can inoculate my client and my case.

We practice until they can answer a simple "yes or no" question, knowing that they will get to explain when I ask them some follow up questions.

WITNESS CREDIBILITY AND ACCURACY

I have written extensively about this in "Burt's Lie Detector," [6] http://hunterlawfirm.net/burts-lie-detector/.

We lawyers must try to gather accurate facts, but WV divorce lawyers do not usually have private investigators at their beck and call. It is essential that we get accurate facts from our clients. I use "Burt's lie detector" and diligent questioning to a point where the evidence that we gather later usually is quite consistent.

It drives me to distraction, lawyers who pontificate, accuse, exaggerate, and fail to test their own clients' credibility. It is a plague on our profession.

DISCOVERY AND DISCLOSURE.

Some lawyers will "hide the ball." For more on this, please see my post, http://hunterlawfirm.net/why-play-by-the-rules/ Such lawyers will answer an interrogatory (written question) on a Monday that they know of no potential witnesses or exhibits, and on Friday, the deadline for filing the witness list, they will suddenly discover that they have 35 witnesses and 66 exhibits! That, my friends, is a disingenuous lawyer!

We can win and play by the rules, so that's what I do. It is the same with documents. We grow our lists as the documents come in, so it is easy to disclose them when the time comes.

IN CLOSING: Please gather those puzzle piece, make your various lists, complete that Timeline, and help you lawyer be the best that he can be, for you.

III.
FAMILY LAW AND COURT

1.   Divorce 101 Handout

Two clients called this week worried about their case management conferences, so here is an informal glossary which I now hand out to new family law clients. (See also my Oct. 5, 2011 blog post at www.burtonhunteresq.blogspot.com.)

A.   The beginning document is filed with the circuit clerk. It is called a Petition.

B.   The Answer must be filed within 20 or 30 days of service (by sheriff or publication, or certified mail).

C.   The person filing first is the Petitioner, and the person answering is the Respondent.

D.   The respondent may file a counter-petition with his/her own accusations, called allegations. It must be filed with the answer.

E.   A "petition for a rule to show cause" is also called a contempt petition. It alleges violation(s) of a court order and must be approved first by the court with an "order filing petition and notice of hearing."

F.   In divorces, several documents must be filed with the petition:

      i.   An affidavit swearing to the truth of the accusations;

ii.   A proposed parenting plan if there are children;

iii.   A detailed financial affidavit of assets (their values), debts (their unpaid balances), and their income;

iv.   Most family courts expect a "one year and two-year caretaking functions worksheet" setting out the litigant's estimation of percentages of time (totaling 100%) of the caretaking functions performed for the child; and,

v.   An application for services from the WV Dept. of Health and Human Resources' Bureau of Child Support Enforcement (which handles child support and alimony payments.

G.   For people who need help fast:

i.   The party seeking relief can file a petition or motion for ex parte relief. If the attached affidavit is compelling, and the risk of irreparable harm apparent, the family court may grant some relief without a hearing. Examples are an order prohibiting taking the child out of state, restraining order, or even temporary custody. More often, the court will deny the immediate relief and set an emergency hearing; and,

ii.   A motion for expedited relief, where the party gets no immediate relief but asks for an early hearing, which most courts will provide.

H. Some Family Court Judges comply with WV Supreme Court time-lines by issuing a Case Management Conference order. The Case Management Conference moves the case along via a short telephone interview of the parties or their counsel, or counsel's paralegal. The court wants to know the mandatory parenting classes have been scheduled and all required documents filed. Often the court will send the parties to mediation with the "CMC Order," set a status hearing date.

I. Other judges issue their own preliminary orders, for pre-mediation screening, the temporary hearing time and date, etc.

J. Mediation is covered extensively in my blog. It is a "non-adversarial form of "alternate dispute resolution." The mediator has received formal training, and must have extensive experience.

K. A temporary order is just what it implies. The court issues an order on temporary custody, child support, alimony, possession of the family residence, possession of property such as a car, a constructive trust of the marital property, or a restraining order. It is very important and often is an harbinger of things to come.

L. A final order is also what the name implies. It is the final ruling of the trial court. It can also hold a party in contempt. It is appealable to the circuit court.

M. Sometimes a case is bifurcated. That is, the divorce might be granted or property awarded, but the custody case might be handled separately and sent to mediation or contested trial. There is no jury. The family court judge is judge and jury (fact-finder).

N.   A property settlement agreement divides and assigns marital debt and property. WV, being "an equitable distribution state," assumes 50%/50% ownership of the marital assets and debts.

O.   An agreed parenting plan, or a court ordered parenting plan, followed by an order incorporating that plan into the court's final decision covers:

    i.   Parenting time, overnight, day time, holidays, and vacations time;

    ii.   Decision making; major non-emergency decisions, emergency decisions, and day to day decisions. Most fit parents have co-equal decision making;

    iii.   Access to records, medical, dental, school, and juvenile;

    iv.   Alternate dispute resolution, usually mediation; and,

    v.   Many other things are in a Permanent Parenting Plan Agreement, such as relocation of a parent, child support, medical insurance and support, alternate care providers, limitations on a parent because of drug or alcohol abuse, physical abuse, dangerous companions, mutual respect, no criticism of the other parent, smoking, custody exchange points and rules, and anything else pertaining to the welfare of the children.

P.   Rules. Your case is governed by many rules:

   i.   Family Court Rules;

   ii.   Rules of Civil Procedure, especially "discovery rules;"

   iii.   Rules of Evidence;

   iv.   Appellate Rules;

   v.   But not the Marquess of Queensberry rules;

   vi.   And, as the drunken brawler told Paul Newman in the classic movie, "There ain't no rules in a knife fight!" We all know what Paul did next. So, be careful out there.

I trust my clients who get this hand-out will be relieved that their lawyer and his staff are going to lead them through this maze! If you have a family law dispute and do not have a lawyer, beware! **Sometimes the other side does not play by the rules!**

2.   **If I Could Know Only Ten Things About My Family Law Case, What Would They Be?**

A.   You probably have a much better understanding of what you are facing in family court than if you had a serious injury claim because your friends may have been through it and you have the WV Supreme Court's "do it yourself" package, but this can lead to over-confidence.

B.   There are huge pitfalls in divorce and custody matters I discuss in my blog articles:

http://hunterlawfirm.net/?p=237

http://hunterlawfirm.net/?p=390

http://hunterlawfirm.net/?p=389

C.   Your case will be governed by:

i.   The Family Court Rules;

ii.   The WV Rules of Civil Procedure;

iii.   The WV Rules of Evidence;

iv.   The WV Rules of Appellate Procedure;

v.   WV Statutes;

vi.   WV Case Law; and

vii.   The quirks and traits of your Family Court Judge.(*Unless you are very determined, you know none of these things!*)

D.   The right lawyer can provide you an invaluable consultation and guide you to these and other important resources for as little as $500. Just a few things you might not know:

i.   There is no such thing as "custody" or "visitation" now.

ii.   The person who buys a particular item during the marriage, or has it titled solely in her name, still has only a 50% ownership, and it usually doesn't matter in whose name the property is titled;

iii. "My retirement" is not just "my" retirement. It is yours equally, and;

iv.   There are very limited conditions where a Grandparent can seek custodial rights for a grandchild.

E.   The lawyer who demands the "big retainer" of $6000-$12,000 may not be right for you! I will tailor the retainer to the percentage of likelihood that the case will, or will not, go to trial. Thus, we can offer equal or better services (we think better) for $1500-$5000 up front retainers. Think of the fellow sitting on that $12,000 pile of cash. Where is the motivation for efficiency and prompt resolution? There is at least an appearance that he might be tempted to make sure several thousand dollars of services are performed before serious settlement efforts are begun. We gladly make partial refunds of retainers, knowing we have another satisfied customer!

F.   What you do not know about mediation and settlement techniques can fill dozens of books. With a good lawyer, 90% of cases settle before a trial. Without one? What do you think? And what happens, as in most divorces, when one party has a power advantage?

G.   Setting aside the fact that you do not know how to question witnesses, prepare exhibits, or get them admitted into evidence, or make appropriate objections to the other side's evidence, there are critical techniques you need to organize the facts in your case. I write about that in:

http://hunterlawfirm.net/?p=381

http://hunterlawfirm.net/?p=279

H.   If you do not get what you want at the trial level, you will have a "double whammy" in that you do not know how to appeal a case, and you probably already screwed up the record by not knowing what to present at trial.

I.   Agreeing to one too many, or too few, overnight visits a month in an agreed parenting plan can cost you thousands of dollars in child support and even prevent, or allow, a parent to move with the child to another state. Think about that!

J.   If you call a lawyer, you are still in control. I never hesitate to give a "free consultation" over the phone. Options exist to pay a consultation fee, or I will give you a firm retainer quote after 15-20 minutes. After hiring the lawyer, you still make the decisions, after getting my advice of course. I have 41 years' experience, and at least 50,000 hours of family law work, available to help you protect your children and your rights.

3. The Divorcing Litigant's Big Argument

The argument for *not* consulting a lawyer in your divorce:

A.   At least half of all lawyers are below average. (I know I am a bit tough on family law lawyers here, but it is the mindset we bring from law school and our lives that I disagree with. There is a movement for a better way, and I hope it will begin to change this concept of "an adversary system.")

B.   Family law tends to attract aggressive people with a high tolerance for conflict.

C.   Lawyers have been trained in "the adversary system." Siri defines "adversary" as "One's opponent in a conflict, contest, or dispute. e.g., The Devil." How crazy is that? The person you swore to love and honor, for your lifetime together, with whom you had children, acquired property, and shared dreams. Now you must sue one another in order to get a divorce! What's a person to do? Good question.

D.   Relatively few family lawyers are innovative, creative, and determined in dispute resolution. Their approach is to argue, threaten, bluster, and fight. It is very tough to be collegial and cooperative with a lawyer exhibiting these behaviors.

E.   Lawyers tend to be expensive, and family law lawyers who are in great demand sometimes cost more than average because of their reputations.

F.   And, "My spouse says he would like to do this 'without lawyers." I hear this quite often.

The argument for consulting *this* particular experienced lawyer in your divorce:

G.   I strongly believe I am not "below average." If you "do your homework" on me and my staff, I am confident you will agree with that assessment.

H.   I am an aggressive person with a high tolerance for conflict who has learned to moderate his natural tendencies for the good of his client and her/his children, while being alert for the "bullies" of the world.

I.   I am doing everything in my power to be innovative, creative, and determined in dispute resolution. I try to reason with my opponents and to "punish" the truly unreasonable lawyers and parties. "Punish" simply means do a good job, try the case vigorously, and get the best results in those cases where the other side simply will not agree to a fair compromise.

J.   My staff and I have innovative methods, and various products, that keep my fees substantially below the "big retainer: see you in Court" lawyers.

K.   There is no better way to "get along," and to avoid being pushed around, than by teaching your spouse that bullying, and pressure will not move you. Your post-divorce will be different than the marriage, with mutual respect, fairness, equity, and placing the children first. Had these things been in full force during the marriage, the divorce might not have been necessary.

L.	The spouse who says "let's do this without lawyers" is often the more aggressive spouse, the one who is sure he can turn you to his will, or the one who sees he/she has more to lose if the other side has a lawyer. If "do this without lawyers" is supposed to mean work out an amicable settlement, I do that at a much higher rate than "average." And "fair" to you does not mean you walk out the door in a barrel with leather shoulder straps! A "good divorce" is an equitable one that maximizes the parties' chances of working together later for the sake of the children.

M.	And, I have negotiated thousands of property settlements and parent plans. How often have you and your spouse done that? And what is your experience and knowledge of "the rules of the divorce game"? There are family court rules, rules of evidence, rules of civil procedure, appellate rules, civil cases, and Supreme Court case precedent. You don't know them, so you need someone who does.

N.	Knowledge is power. For a "consultation fee" of $500, I can evaluate your case, gather a history, provide options, discuss fee arrangements, and empower you. We are not too expensive, aggressive, or too adversarial for most working people. And we will help you guide your behavior for your best interests and your children.

O.	At the end of that interview, all of your options remain on the table, but your information base will be much larger. Contact me at *304-472-7477;* hunterjb@hunterlawfirm.net

4. "Legal Disability" - What Do a Soldier, a 17-Year-Old, an Inmate, and a Hospitalized Mental Patient Have in Common?

The idea for this article came from my trusty paralegal, Letetia. She suggested I touch on some ramifications of an infant's personal injury settlement.

That did not seem to have a very broad appeal, and then I realized the concept of "legal incompetency," or "being under a legal disability," has a huge bearing on all aspects of our legal system. Voila! An idea was born.

A few synonyms for "competent" are *capable, proficient, adroit, accomplished, complete, skillful, gifted,* and *talented.* I like to apply these terms to myself and my staff!

So, what goes with my question above? I have known some very competent teenagers, soldiers, hospital patients, and even prisoners. The "trick" is that "competent" is a term of art when it refers to "legal competence," or "being under a legal disability."

And there are different kinds of "legal competence." For example, there is a "presumption" that a 14-year-old is "competent" to testify in court under oath and a presumption that a child under 7 is not. Yet both are under legal disabilities be virtue of being "an infant," that is being less than 18 years old.

What I refer to here when I say "incompetent" is a person under a "legal disability."

Here are some examples:

A.   The Federal "Service Members' Civil Relief Act" provides protections to an active duty military member who may be unable to protect her/his legal rights. It would hardly be fair for a person to have a large money judgment rendered against them, or to lose custody, while defending his country in Iraq or Afghanistan, or guarding the border in Korea.

B.   An incarcerated person is unable to protects her/his legal rights. They can't even vote.

C.   A person who is elderly, in a coma, a stroke victim, or mentally ill, may be incompetent to make medical or financial decisions.

D.   An "infant" is defined as incompetent because they cannot enter into certain contracts, sign personal injury releases, file civil suits, or conduct certain kinds of business transactions.

So, how does the law deal with such "incompetency"?

E.   If a person is under a "legal disability" for one of the reasons listed above, for example a divorce, the court will often appoint the person a *guardian ad litem*. A guardian, under law, acts in some ways as the person's lawyer. There are funds available through the WV Supreme Court of Appeals Administrator to pay for such services.

F.   If an "infant" has parents who have custody, the parent(s) may file as "next friend" and guardian, for example, in a personal injury law suit.

G.   Where a person has not executed a "medical power of attorney" but becomes unable to make medical decisions, the State of WV has a "medical surrogacy" law to assist the medical provider to determine who can make medical decisions.

H.   Where a person has become "elderly and infirm" or otherwise is going to be impaired for the foreseeable future, WV has a "Guardian and Conservator Statute." The person applying for this position must comply with the statute, take an online course and pass, notice all close relatives, get a statement from the patient's doctor, and file a "verified (notarized) petition." If appointed, they must also file periodic reports and perhaps post a bond.

I.   As a *fiduciary* the person acting as guardian and conservator must adhere to very high standards and place their ward's interests above their own. There are borderline cases where a person has not been declared incompetent, but someone has been helping them with their finances. If that fiduciary, perhaps by using a power of attorney or joint account, benefits monetarily, he or she may have to overcome the "presumption of fraud" if suit is later filed to get the money back.

J.   Search my blog (www.hunterlawfirm.net) for related topics such as "general power of attorney," "medical power of attorney," or "special power of attorney."

K.   Even where a suit has not been filed, a parent who wants to settle his/her child's personal injury suit must file a petition for an "infant's summary proceeding" and convince the court that taking the settlement and releasing the tortfeasor (also called "defendant" of part of a lawsuit) from all further liability. It is the same principal if the injured party is mentally incompetent, for example, by a brain injury.

L. Without the order approving settlement, the insurance company is not going to write that check! These cases also require appointment of a guardian ad litem, usually paid for by the insurance company. It is the guardian's job to make sure the settlement is fair for the injury and extent of liability. The guardian's responsibility is to the infant or impaired person.

M. The question that Letetia wanted me to answer is, "What if the infant wants some of the money now?" Answer? Usually the money is for the child to receive at adulthood. It may not be used by the parent in lieu of supporting the child. That's already the parents' responsibility.

N. The court has to approve the purchase of a car for the child to get to work or a computer for school use, or for the first year of college. My experience is the courts are not well disposed to such requests. It is a case by case issue.

O. Where the injuries are severe and the settlement large, the parent often considers accepting a "structured settlement," especially if they doubt their child, at 18, can handle that much money.

P. Such a settlement may include an initial lump sum, less attorney fees based on the "present value" of the settlement, and periodic, monthly, quarterly, or annual payments. Sometimes the payments are timed to correspond to high school graduation, anticipated time the person may want to marry or build a house, etc.

Q.   Sometimes a parent will take and get the court to approve a "structure" so the child will not have the money to "blow" upon turning 18. And believe me they do sometimes "blow it."

R.   Unfortunately, there are plenty of companies that will buy a structured settlement from that 18-year-old for a flat fee and pay all tax and other liabilities. They charge a heavy premium for that service.

S.   You may also search for "means tested benefits," where a person gets a settlement but is receiving government benefits that are tied to their meeting certain "poverty guidelines." That is a separate subject, but the recipient is under a form of "disability" because if they just take the money, they may be knocked off their SSI, Medicaid, food stamps, or other benefits, until all settlement proceeds are "spent down."

T.   In such an event, a proceeding similar in complexity to a guardianship/conservatorship petition, or infant summary proceeding, must be conducted seeking approval of a "special needs trust." If approved, a court appointed trustee can pay for certain needs of the beneficiary such as therapy, assisted living, treatment at a wellness clinic, or a new roof.

Of course, there are borderline cases, such as where a person had dementia, with resultant short-term memory problems, but who appears able to understand what they owe and own, where and who they are, and what they want. Thus, some of these cases can be contested, especially when those affected begin to "smell the money" of the supposedly impaired person.

In the "special needs trust" petitions I have filed, I have had the WV Attorney General and the WV Department of Health and Human Resources resist the petition because of the "WV Rules." These can include the beneficiary's being over 59 or being otherwise disqualified.

In Summary, a person who is disqualified, by law or fact, must be treated carefully by our legal system if justice is to be served.

This is not the kind of thing a person can handle without competent legal counsel.

5. How Do I Modify My Child Custody Order?

This is a question I am asked around 25 times a year. First, what is a parenting plan? From at least the time when the legislature did away with the "primary caretaker rule," which usually favored the Mother in custody cases, parties have been encouraged to fashion "shared parenting plans" under which to raise their children.

Seminar speakers at the time assured us that the new rule would have very little impact in the "real world." They were wrong, and I tend to think more good has been done by the new rules than bad.

Under the old standards, one parent "won custody" or was awarded custody, and the other parent was the "absent parent" entitled to "visitation" and access to the children's (school, medical, and juvenile) records via a "consent" signed by the "custodial parent."

The inequity of such rules is apparent to me now, although back then I took comfort that the parent who had been more involved in the children's lives maintained "control."

The term "major non-emergency decisions" means decisions made relative to medical treatment, schooling, extra-curricular activities, and religious upbringing. The "non-custodial parent" could rage over the administration of the asthma medicine or Ritalin for ADHD, and some even sneaked their children to another Dr. during the week-ends, but it was far from a healthy situation. One parent kept "control," and the other was clearly "second class." Often the Court referred to that parent as the "absent parent." Father's and men's rights organizations were militantly against that status quo.

Under the shared parenting concept, "fit parents" usually have equal access to records and co-equal decision making, on **"the major non-emergency decisions."**

With each parent having a veto over **"major non-emergency decisions," you might think there would be constant stalemate. NOT TRUE**. Things have become much better. Now that the "non-residential" parent can speak with the pediatrician, the coach, and the Sunday school teacher, and have a say in major decisions, there is less contention. Having the right to drag the other parent to the mediator, at a shared cost usually leads to a compromise solution. Of course, one of the parents usually ends up making these decisions more than the other but having "the right" to share in the decision seems to ameliorate some of the resentment and distrust. I often urge parents to go talk with the teacher or doctor together.

Most parenting plans in North Central WV result from agreements achieved at mediation. When parents cannot agree, the Court decides.

BUT, what happens when one party is unhappy with a parenting plan? Each year I see a dozen or so "pro se" Petitions to Modify Parenting Plan. "Pro se" is another term for "self-represented." So far, not one of the pro se petitions states a case under existing statutes. That means they should be thrown out immediately, but our Family Courts have been too intimidated by recent WV Supreme Court rulings requiring them to excuse away the mistakes of pro se litigants. That's a bit of an exaggeration, but it can be frustrating to an attorney to make an objection or file a motion that would be sustained or granted, BUT FOR the fact the other party is representing herself or himself.

The modification statutes are in WV Code Article 48, Chapter 9, Section 401, "Modification upon Showing of Changed Circumstances or Harm," and Section 402, "Modification Without Showing of Changed Circumstances."

The old standard was, simply, "Material Change in Circumstances." But, when the judges returned from their judicial training, the full import of these statutes became clear fairly rapidly. Judges use them as an excuse NOT to do the hard work of tailoring parenting plans to the best interests of the children. Truth is, they do not have time.

Section 402 allows modification if:

A.   **The parents agree** and the Court determines the agreement is knowing and voluntary, and not harmful to the children;

B.   There is NOT a material change in circumstances but the parties have been following a different (de facto) plan continuously, and voluntarily, for six months;

C.   The modification constitutes a "minor modification" of the plan;

D.   When modification is necessary to accommodate the reasonable and firm preferences of a child who has attained the age of 14; and

E.   Modification can be granted when the other parent has made repeated filings of fraudulent reports of domestic violence or child abuse.

There is also case law that one parent's withholding of the child from the other may be a basis for a transfer of custody.

Modification based on "substantial and material change in circumstances" means facts which arose since the entry of the prior custody order, which were not known at the time of the entry, and were not anticipated by the parties, such as Mom's new boyfriend's opening a meth lab in her garage!

We try not to use the terms "custody" and "visitation" preferring the more benign "shared parenting" and "time with the child." But, we know old habits die hard.

Realizing that single moms are often at a disadvantage in funds and resources, the legislature further determined that "choice of reasonable caretaking arrangements, including day care" would not be a "material change".

Nor is a parent's remarriage or cohabitation a "material change.

West Virginia is the State which had a nationally famous "Gay Parent Case," *In Re: Clifford K.* That case motivated the "Kansas Krazies" to demonstrate in Buckhannon on the campus of WV Wesleyan College, during the Sago Miners' Memorial Service.

In *Clifford K,* **the WV Supreme Court awarded custody of a five-year-old child to the surviving lesbian partner of a biological mother** killed in an auto collision. The Court ruled that she was the child's "psychological parent", which, of course, she was. It carefully defined and delineated when a person claiming to be a "psychological parent" can participate in litigation seeking primary or other custodial rights of a child.

Grandparents' rights to visitation have been limited by a U.S. Supreme Court Decision. And the question of grandparent's gaining custody is a complex and changing one. **(Note: a recent case, In Re Haylea G. 231 W.Va. 494, 745 S.E.2nd 532 (2013), has turned the advantage back to biological parents in all but the most egregious situations.)**

The WV guardianship statute appears to be gaining in use, perhaps as an easier route than the "psychological parent," when parents become unable to care for the child but the resources of the WV Department of Human Resources, Child Protective Services Department just can't keep pace with the workload.

The point of all this is that WV Family Courts now try to apply a formula to Petitions for Modification, and it is clearly an area of the law that one should not try to traverse without a good attorney. Being a "good lawyer", my bias is

53

clear, but my views are based on sound logic. Until one understands how judges look at this subject, he/she does not have a chance of successfully pursuing a petition to modify a parenting plan.

6. The Maze of WV Child Custody Issues: Just Dropping Cookies Won't Get You Out

This isn't going to be an easy read, but if you were going to try to get through the Amazon jungle, naked, wouldn't you at least like to talk to a guide first?

First: some history:

A.   Fast forward from the time when men controlled the lives of their wives and children. Think Abraham, who in the Old Testament the Lord asked to sacrifice his son; Henry the VIII who imprisoned and beheaded his wife and banished another; or fundamentalist Islamic lack of women's rights and revenge killings of own family members.

B.   When I arrived to the practice of law, there was a presumption that children should stay with their mother, visit with Dad every other weekend or so, and receive child support. That idea came from Victorian England and the idealization of women and mothers.

C.   Then our Supreme Court, followed by our legislature, came up with the "primary caretaker" rule, to the effect that the person who provided "the majority of caretaking" during the marriage "won custody". She got "full custody", and the "loser", called the "absent parent", got something called "visitation" and paid "child support", and the "absent parent" only got access to their children's records; juvenile, school, medical, if the "custodial parent" would sign a permission form, which of course she would not do unless court ordered.

D.   It was very comforting when the Mother had done the vast majority of caretaking, was a good mother and person, and the father was controlling or abusive; but not so much when mother was a mediocre parent, vindictive, an alcoholic, drug addict, or had not bonded with the child. It was rare for a father to be named "primary caretaker". Dad was stuck with the term "breadwinner" but not "custody winner".

E.   Several years ago, a new rule came into being pursuant to WV Code Sec. 48-9-206. If both parents were fit, the court, subject to some exceptions, was expected to figure out who had performed what percentage of "caretaking functions". At the temporary hearing, the court was to look back one year, and at the final hearing the court was to look back two years.

F.   It was, and is, still slanted in favor of a stay-at-home or part time employed parent, but this lawyer believes that more often than not in WV one parent is more nurturing and "hands on," and it is, barring fitness issues such as drugs, alcohol, or mental illness, the mother. That's my experience from 46 years of being a lawyer.

G.   I was startled recently when a family court announced that the caretaking functions history of the parties is the least important factor that it considers, and in spite of dangerous, felonious, and abusive behavior of one of the parents, awarded the parties 50%/50% time with a two-year-old female child. I have only encountered one court with this view, but perhaps that's the wave of the future, and it scares me. It smacks of deciding a case BEFORE the evidence is presented.

You may want to stop here and come back later. zzzzzzzzzzzzzzzzzzz......

You are probably reading now because you had a nice nap, or you have a problem and are seeking a solution. Here are some of them.

The combinations are myriad.

A. Short marriage with young children;

B. Longer marriage with teenagers;

C. Unmarried couple, some who lived together for quite a while, so the "caretaking functions" rule applies, and some who had what is known as a "one-night stand";

D. A married couple, and a biological parent who has consented to an adoption, or "abandoned" the child so the stepfather can adopt;

E. A single parent whose spouse or partner has died or become "impaired." Now his parents want his/their "rights";

F. A grandparent, homosexual step-parent, family friend, court approved foster parent, or relative who has raised the child for several years and who the child considers to be his/her parent. That's called a "psychological parent";

G.	In "5." above, the biological parent(s) can be any combination of

H.	Dead;

I.	Unfit because of drug abuse or alcohol addiction;

J.	Homeless, or mentally impaired; or

K.	A respondent in a juvenile abuse and neglect proceeding in circuit court.

Got that? Great! There are many more combinations, but these give you an idea.

Let me try to confuse you a bit more.

A.	Magistrate court issues temporary domestic violence protective orders that then go to family court.

B.	And they can start a juvenile case which is then heard by the circuit court. More on juvenile abuse and neglect later.

C.	Family court "shares jurisdiction" with circuit courts, and circuit courts are the appellate court for the family courts. Got it?

D.	Family court, among other things, hears the domestic violence cases that start in magistrate court. These are "restraining order" cases that activate The Federal Gun Control Act and last from 90 to 365 days. During that period, the respondent may not possess a firearm. These cases are not criminal cases, but violations of DV orders CAN result in incarceration and criminal charges. And they carry a big stigma. Think "wife beater."

E.   Misdemeanor charges of assault or battery are criminal, and heard by magistrate court, and more serious cases, malicious wounding, attempted murder, etc. are criminal cases, heard by the circuit cases, and are not dealt with in this article.

F.   Family courts also hear what used to be called "paternity cases", which are now, "Petitions For Allocation Of Parental Rights". Thanks to DNA testing, the salacious factual disputes have been eliminated. What a pain it was dealing with who did what, with whom, and how often?

G.   These cases can be instituted by the mother or putative father. I know one where the mother filed "an allocation petition" against one man, and her other boyfriend filed an allocation petition against her and the respondent in the other case. She kept telling each, "You're the guy!"

H.   Family courts hear almost all divorces, including parenting issues, equitable distribution of assets and debts, children's issues, non-domestic violence restraining orders, alimony, and attorney's fees. When parties negotiate successfully, family court approves parenting plan agreements and property settlement agreements.

I discuss "non-domestic violence" restraining orders in two previous blog articles, and I encourage you to read them. One is "Senate Bill 430: The Bill No One Heard of," http://wp.me/p4utce-tH . The other is "WV

Families Dodge a Metaphorical Bullet," http://wp.me/p4utce-v7 The short version is the WV Supreme Court of Appeals took away from family courts the power to restrain bad behavior that fell short of domestic violence, but easily could spiral into violence. This bill restored the court's power in this vital regard. That bill, which I co-authored, is "The Family Court Restraining Order" Act, WV Code 51-2A-2a.

There is a critter called a "guardianship action". These involve children and are distinct from petitions for guardianship/conservatorship of incompetent or disabled adults. Infant guardianship petitions are filed in the office of the clerk of the circuit court. Contested guardianships are usually heard by circuit courts even though they "share jurisdiction" with family courts. Some circuit courts remand the cases to be heard by the family court judge.

Phew! Break time! ....

I. Circuit courts now have a huge workload of juvenile abuse and neglect cases. These cases are instituted by Child Protective Services Division of the WV Dept. of Health and Human Resources, WVDHHR/CPS, via the county prosecuting attorney.

J. Abuse and neglect cases are a world of their own. I visit there only when my family cases "spill over." My current such case is approaching two years' old. It involves a dreaded creature called "the MDT"! Also known as "the multidisciplinary team".

59

K.   When one of the parents is fit, that parent can be a co-petitioner with the State. My experience is that fathers are second hand citizens in these courts, often because fathers are uninvolved parents, but also because of pre-conceptions of the people who populate this system.

Huge factors in all these cases are:

Drugs;

Alcohol;

Drugs;

Domestic violence;

Drugs;

Poverty

Drugs

Mental Health issues, and;

Did I mention drugs?

My personal observation is that in family court the presumption is a parent is fit, and in "abuse and neglect", circuit court, the assumption is the offending parent is not. And woe be it if you piss off or become averse to the CPS worker, the prosecutor, the court appointed lawyer for the child (guardian ad litem) or, woe of woes, all of the above! Do everything, and I mean everything you can, to ingratiate yourself with these people if you want a good result.

Adoptions can be consensual, where biological parent(s) sign(s) a relinquishment of parental rights. But don't think you can relinquish rights and avoid child support. One cannot relinquish until there is another parent lined up to assume those responsibilities.

"Grandparents issues" can be a simple petition for grandparent visitation, or a full-blown guardianship (custody) petition including the claim the grandparent is a "psychological parent".

In most cases, fit parents are "the deciders" relative to grandparents' rights. The statute is WV Code Sec. 48-10-101. Major issues happen when the child of the grandparent dies or becomes impaired or incarcerated, and the custodial parent feels threatened or controlled by his/her parents.

The "psychological parent" case, *In Re: Clifford K,* defined the parameters of actions brought by people who claim to stand in the shoes of a parent. Such people are not allowed simply to file an action. They must move to intervene in existing actions. I have a combination of allegations that I include in such cases, which an opponent recently labeled "a mishmash" of allegations.

I do whatever I can, within the law, to give the court the facts upon which to hang a decision based on the welfare of the child, which is supposed to be the "polar star" that guides the court. But sometimes things called "presumptions" do away with a requirement that certain facts be proved.

I have written an article, "Digging Down: On Organizing the Facts in Your Case," http://wp.me/p4utce-mr which describes my system for helping clients to organize the facts in their cases in order to provide me a "complete history" of relevant facts. It is a "nuts and bolts" description which I believe empowers my client to assume considerable responsibility to keep attorney fees within reasonable bounds.

The resources of all these courts are finite, so presentation of the evidence must be targeted, concise, and effective. At the early stages, "proffers" of anticipated evidence summarize effectively in just a few minutes. Presenting good proffers takes practice and experience.

Most cases are not "saved" by closing argument, as the court pretty much has it figured out by then.

A good lawyer is pragmatic and realistic. He or she must be passionate but not overly-zealous. The lawyer who helps you lie and cheat, is, well, a liar and cheater, and he or she will do the same to you.

The best lawyers care more for your children than they do for you. And they "work, work, work" to help the client improve as a person and overcome personal weaknesses. One of the better compliments a court appointed "guardian ad litem", lawyer for the child, gave me is "You give your client every opportunity to succeed". I hope that is true and try to make sure it is.

When I see the client is going to lose, I do everything I can to limit the damage. It is stressful and emotional.

I cannot conclude without urging to have the right lawyer for the job and not to think you can handle a case of any import on your own based on your own standards of right and wrong and common sense. Do that, and even a good case can "go down the tubes". I hope these words have given you insights into the subject that most people know as "child custody".

7. Most of My Clients Have Property Smaller Than the Former Vanderbilt Abode in Asheville, N.C., The Biltmore!

There seems to be less confusion about the basics of equitable distribution than other aspects of WV divorce law. Most people who come to me understand that property acquired by the work of either party during the marriage is presumed to be owned 50%/50%. As they say, "The devil is in the details."

That doesn't mean they are happy about it. The man especially does not want his estranged wife to have "half of MY retirement". Many think their stay-at-home wife should walk away with nothing. Perhaps that is an insight as to why they are facing a divorce!

Strong marriages often have a shared assumption that everything is shared by both parties equal! But, when a wealthy person marries a pauper, or people in their 40's-60's with adult children and other complications marry, the ramifications can be much different than when two people of similar status marry young.

WV is an "equitable distribution state," not a "community property state."

Here is a practical (instead of scholarly) explanation:

A.   If it was purchased during the marriage, whether by one person's paycheck or both, whether titled in one or both names, and even if it's lottery winnings from a ticket bought from a cashed paycheck, it is marital.

B. If it was inherited by, deeded to, or gifted to the recipient only, by a friend or family member, it is separate.

C. If separate property such as cash is deposited into a joint account, or conveyed 50% by deed to the other spouse, it usually is treated as a completed gift or conveyance of half of that property. So, now it is marital.

D. If separate property, e.g., the family house owned by a party before the wedding, is secured by a loan, incurred before or during the marriage, and that marital debt is paid off during the marriage with marital income, the increase in the value of the equity is considered marital, and, until that equity becomes as valuable as the separate property, the equity and the separate property are considered "mixed" property. Examples of "mixed" property are:

   i.   The log cabin on 50 acres, inherited from husband's grandmother, that the parties spent $100,000 improving, incurring an $80,000 loan. The "marital" part is the increased value of the property, NOT the amount spent, which might be much more. Editor's Note: this example requires a dual calculation, the reduction of debt by loan payments made during the marriage, and the increase in value by the investment of marital income. Passive increases in value of separate property are not supposed to become marital.

   ii. The real estate becomes marital as that debt is paid off and equity increases. If the other

$20,000 came from separate property of a spouse, there is some law supporting the concept that the contributing person can ask for a variance from the 50%/50% rule, but the stronger law presumes it as a gift too.

iii.   The example in b. above is "fact driven;" for example, if the spouse who owns nothing in the cabin expresses doubt about investing $100,000 into the other spouse's cabin, and promises are exchanged (and perhaps a fence built) assuring the reluctant spouse that if he will agree to incur the loan and pay the payments, that five acres will be carved out around the cabin and a right of way to and from it created as marital property, the spouse who made that promise will likely be "estopped" from refusing to sign a deed to that five acres later.

iv.   The better course of action is to agree in writing (in order to avoid misunderstandings) and get the deed signed before the construction begins. But, people in love do not always act in their best financial interests, and some promises are soon forgotten. Editor's note: The other side of this coin is negotiating a pre-nuptial agreement at the beginning of a marriage can lead to tension and resentment that leads to marital strife, even the cancelling of the wedding.

v.   Where a party works 15 years, building a retirement, before marriage, marries, and divorces 25 years after that, the general rule is the spouse shares 50% of the retirement accumulated during those 25 years.

vi.   The "simple calculation" is to divide 25 years by 40 years and to split the result evenly: 25/40 = 62.5%; 62.5%/2 = 31.25%. Thus, the spouse is entitled to just under 1/3 of the 40-year fund. The 25/40 is called the "marital coverture."

vii.   Our WV Supreme Court ruled in 2006, "50% really means 50%", when it ruled that the stay-at-home wife of the dog racing mogul, whose marital estate was worth over $26,000,000.00, really was entitled to $13,000,000.00. That case is Arneault v. Arneault, 639 S.E.2d 720 (2006).

viii.   The facts that she stayed at home, raised the children, ran the house, entertained guests, including business associates, and managed household finances, which were considerable, were sufficient to show an agreed marital partnership. Barring extreme hardship, that's the assumption the court is going to make, especially if to do otherwise would result in a gender preference.

ix.   Methods of rebutting the marital presumption include proof of gambling addiction, alcoholism, or drug addiction that reduce the marital estate, or just plain stupid-wasted or misjudgment. I once had a case where my client, a title abstracter, came home and warned the husband that his friends had a number of tax liens recorded against them. She urged him to have no business dealings with them. He ignored her, co-signed on their loan, and that debt was determined to be separate.

x.   Another twist is when the marital residence is built on the in-law's property, based on assurances the lot will be theirs. Later (They always knew he was a bum!), the parties separate, and the promises to convey the land are rescinded, forgotten, or denied. This scenario is also "fact driven," and the litigation must move to the circuit court since it involves parties who are not part of the marital partnership. Often these issues are resolved at mediation since neither party relishes the expense or delay of another lawsuit, in circuit court, involving one of the party's parents.

xi.   A gift to parties before the marriage fails is just that. The giver doesn't get to take it back if the spouse is a louse. Thus, a couch that both used, the washer/dryer, and the van put in both names, are marital, but the personal gifts from family, the engraved rifle, or the deed in daughter's name only, remain separate.

E. **PLEASE NOTE:** I recently was exposed to a VERY IMPORTANT twist to the rules and examples listed in A-K above. In two cases, a spouse disposed of a residence for which they had a good argument were their separate or almost fully separate, property. They signed deeds without notifying their spouse or having their spouse sign the deed. There is a law covering that. It was authored, at least in part, by a friend and colleague of mine, who explained it to me.

It is WV Code Article 43, Chapter 1, Section 2: The rule of the statute is that failure to do either, notice or signature on deed, if done within five years of a divorce creates a conclusive presumption that the property is marital. In one case, that added $100,000 to my client's claim to the former family residence that was titled in the other spouse's name!

Lessons learned from equitable distribution can be hard ones, just as picking the wrong spouse can be one of life's most difficult decisions.

Many people begin to think of getting a pre-nuptial agreement, a subject for another day. My case of *Lee v. Lee, 721 SE 2d 53 (2011)* reveals some of the perils of negotiating your own parenting plan. Both parties here lost because they used a downloaded Internet form!

My thoughts for most West Virginians, even ones who have gained some years, and some property, if you understand the principles below, you just need to make good decisions, to consult your lawyer when it is time to make these decisions, and to manage your property with common sense and compassion.

Good luck. And try to marry the right person, for the right reason(s).

8. You Have Your (Child Custody) Agreement: Now What?

Note: This article was inspired by a nervous client who concedes the parenting plan we negotiated for her is a pretty good one, but who knows it will be violated. That was the path of their last mediated agreement, with the result they were back in court within six months! Is there a path to avoid that? Often there is, and most people do not take it! Here we go:

All too often, a mediator and the parties' lawyers guide the parties to an agreement by predicting the likely rulings of the court, describing existing law, and nudging them in the right direction. But what about enforcement, just making parenting plans work?

Typical violations are the failure of a parent to participate in counseling or take the required video parenting class, failure to keep the other party informed on matters directly relating to the child's welfare, failure to exercise the time that they asked for strongly during mediation, and poor communication, including insults and accusations.

Of course there are also "the big three": substance abuse, alcohol abuse, and domestic violence. I will save them for another post. This post is for functioning adults who can have a successful parenting plan if both want it.

While I have always done some of the things set out below, I pull some ideas together here, so my client, and others like her, will not be back in court in six months!

I urge my client to read and take to heart my two posts "Winning Your Child Custody Case" http://hunterlawfirm.net/the-secrets-to-winning-custody-of-your-child/ and "The Secrets Winning, Number II" http://hunterlawfirm.net/the-secrets-of-winning-number-ii/ .

At the heart of those articles, and my 19 recommendations, is the great wisdom of "The Golden Rule", "Do unto others as you would have others do unto you".

I explain to my client that transparency is essential. If she is going to travel out of the State of WV for a short vacation, or even a trip to Kennywood, and swears the child to silence because she doesn't want to have grief with the other side, grief she will get as soon as he learns of the deception. It is better to deal with such things head-on, and it is forbidden to order your child to keep secrets.

By keeping the other parent informed, preferably in writing, of every important aspect of the child's life, goodwill will be generated, and a record compiled if needed for court.

Kindness often generates reciprocal kindness, but when it does not, the pattern can be seen and proven to the court in subsequent proceedings.

Assuming the client has read the "winning" articles and absorbed my way of approaching problem solving (search "Digging Down" in my blog), here are my tips for the person who is expecting trouble:

Read, understand, commit to memory, and keep with you, your written parenting plan or court order.

Please be sure your attorney gave you copies of the "modification statutes", which have very specific requirements. http://hunterlawfirm.net/how-can-i-get-my-childrens-parenting-plan-modified/

With a difficult person, always communicate in writing, by text, or email, and in certain situations "snail mail". Save those communications. Do not ever let any of them disappear into the ether. Even irrelevant things, if missing, will take on a sinister aspect.

We have begun to utilize the app "My Family Wizard", which can be found at: https://www.ourfamilywizard.com/por/courts, and in two instances my client has reported that she likes it. It allows for uploading of medical records and school class assignments, coordinating transfer points, documenting communication, setting of doctors and dentist appointments, etc. Everything goes through "The Wizard."

Do not let violations slip by, but do not overreact. If the other parent shows up 10 or 15 minutes late to transfer points two or three times, write a formal email "Dear _ _ _, dated _ _ _, Sincerely, your name."

Don't threaten or bluster; cite to your parenting plan and ask her or him to comply. And track in your journal or "The Wizard" whether they do.

Repeat and serious violations should generate a letter, but send it regular mail and certified mail with a return receipt card, with a document clipped to the back called a "certificate of service" certifying that you sent the attached letter by regular mail and certified mail, and keep the return receipt card.

If the other side refuses to accept the letter, but the regular mail does not come back, the court will conclude that they received it. That is why I always send formal communication with both mail types with the certificate of service.

If the violations continue, send another letter, again cite the violation by page and paragraph, but quote the "alternate dispute resolution mechanism", mediation, and tell the other side that one more violation will cause you to schedule mediation, which will cost you each $'s!

If problems persist, activate the "mediation provision". Note: You will have to figure out the proper balance of patience, persistence, and action. The key is to act timely and appropriately at each step. And you will have to follow the right procedures to schedule and notice mediation.

My best estimate is that out of 50 recent contempt cases, I did not find five people who activated the mediation provision before they came back to me. What are people thinking?! The parenting plan is written to be followed, but to be followed by both sides!

You may decide to attend mediation without a lawyer, but the best $500 you can ever spend is a $500 "robust consultation" with a good lawyer (me) reviewing your actions to date, making sure you have documentation, and deciding whether to give the other side "just one more chance".

Of course, serious acts such as child abuse or sexual abuse require immediate action such as reporting at the Child Protective Services, taking the child to the emergency room, filing an emergency ex parte petition or motion for expedited relief, and even reporting the offense to the police.

IN SUMMARY, you must have your own plan if you want your court ordered parenting plan to work. But do everything in the spirit of "The Golden Rule."

Resources for further reading:

http://hunterlawfirm.net/wp-content/uploads/2017/02/BurtsMessages1.jpg

http://hunterlawfirm.net/the-secrets-to-winning-custody-of-your-child/

http://hunterlawfirm.net/the-secrets-of-winning-number-ii

http://hunterlawfirm.net/how-can-i-get-my-childrens-parenting-plan-modified/

https://www.ourfamilywizard.com/por/courts

9.   The Secrets to "Winning" Custody of Your Child

This provocative title of this two-part article is true, but with a twist. There are "secrets" to a winning parenting plan. They start with "The Golden Rule".

For purpose of this article, "winning" has a narrow, but important, definition. I think winning is a happy, emotionally healthy, child, not just the number of "overnights" with the child or amount of child support!

There are, as of this writing, two pending bills in the WV legislature that would change what the lay person considers "custody". I don't think they will pass, but they raised some interesting issues which I touch on below.

If you have 1/2 hour, you can get background on "custody" and its replacement, "parenting", in two of my blog articles.

Several years ago, in an effort to equalize the rights of fathers and mothers and reduce the adversarial nature of what some people still call "custody fights", the legislature replaced "custody" with the concept "shared parenting" (shared but not necessarily co-equal time), and replaced "visitation" with "time with the child".

That statute requires the family court to make findings as to the percentage of caretaking functions each parent, or a third party, did before their separation, and follow those percentages as a guide to time allocation in the court-ordered parenting plan.

Courts are also supposed to disregard temporary, post-separation arrangements, because these are often artificial and against the wishes of one of the parents.

I noticed in the most recent proposed bill, WV SB 243, a provision that will reward the parent most likely to keep the other person informed and involved in the child's life. I sort of like that.

For this article, I think it is a good idea for a separating or divorcing parent to assume that IS the rule and act accordingly, even though I doubt that particular bill will pass.

If the court is going to reward the parent most willing to involve the other parent, I have tips on how to "win" on that issue.

One caveat: there are lots of substandard parents, people who were not born with the gene of compassion, or raised in a way to nurture compassion and empathy. Some of them are dangerous and abusive, and some are   drug or alcohol dependent, or all three! All efforts to "involve" such parents will fail, but giving them the information will bolster the position of the parent who does it.

This article is written primarily for the large majority of divorcing parents, who cannot stay together but who love their children. If you are interested in the particulars of my recommendations, just go to my next blog article, published concurrently with this one; "The Secrets to Winning II;" [3]http://hunterlawfirm.net/the-secrets-of- winning-number-ii/

These are my background articles on custody in West Virginia:

http://hunterlawfirm.net/the-maze-of-wv-child-custody-issues-just-droppi ng-crumbs-wont-get-you-out/, and; http://hunterlawfirm.net/house-bill-2658-the-one-size-fits-all-children- can-go-to-hell-custody-law/

As well as,

A.   http://hunterlawfirm.net/wp-content/uploads/2017/02/BurtsMessages1.jpg

B.   http://wp.me/p4utce-Gr

C.   http://hunterlawfirm.net/the-secrets-of-winning-number-ii/

D.   http://hunterlawfirm.net/the-maze-of-wv-child-custody-issues-just-dropping-crumbs-wont-get-you-out/

E.   http://hunterlawfirm.net/house-bill-2658-the-one-size-fits-all-children-can-go-to-hell-custody-law/

10.   A Review of the Document Assembly Application Pathagoras

I was asked to submit a review for use by the Technolawyer website and resource. I hope I make the cut, but when I finished I realized I had a new blog post! Here it is. My focus is not the "bells and whistles" but the functionality and customer support. Try it, you'll like it.

Re: Pathagoras Review

www.Pathagoras.com

I am a former user of HotDocs and a board member of the WV Association for Justice and WV State Bar. I got tired of losing all my "proprietary" templates every time HotDocs came out with a new version. I couldn't share templates, training was primarily all-day seminars ($800!), and I just got tired of it.

Then I Googled "document assembly" and found Pathagoras and its inventor, Roy Lasris. I consider Roy to be "a friend", which is not something I can say about Bill Gates or the head of Apple. I can reach out to Roy, and he responds. How great is that?

Here's my secret. I usually don't use the full featured 800-page Pathagoras Manual. The basic manual and the "seven-day plan" are much more helpful for me, but similar to the 75 page HotDocs user's manual, which was my only HotDocs resource.

Pathagoras' "help" is like a pyramid: solid useful, information at the top, and a broad base of detailed information as you grow into it.

I know that if I need to "dig down", the "big manual", or Pathagoras' video tutorials, are there for me to search; and, even better, Roy is most accommodating in helping me solve my problems. We've had at least a dozen remote sessions over the years where he has trained me and my staff.

Example? I had a clunky method for listing children in my divorce Petitions and Parenting Plans. I had to say "no" to the name and date of each of the unused or empty variables ([ ]) I had for the names and birth dates of the parties' children. I had spaces for up to six.

After one conference with Roy, I had a sleek "cumulative" feature, which I see he now has included in the application. Now you just select the number of children and have no more work than to add the names/dates of birth for that number of kids. Before I had to say "no" to up to 10 empty variables of name and D.O.B. That's 30 seconds saved for each document.

I know that I could wring even more from this robust document assembly product, but the point of this review is that I don't have to. I go with what works for me. I am busy, and I am no programmer, but I have a working knowledge of Microsoft Office Pro and Word. It's important that you or your staff have that.

If you are a collaborative lawyer, and you should be, form a small community, trade forms, and learn from one another. If not, save it all for yourself.

If you are good at what you do, have a good set of forms for your practice area, and give some thought to decent office systems, this product is for you.

If, after you have used the products for six months, created a number of usable forms, and want to move to "libraries", "dropdown lists", macros, and the rest, go for it! Many of you will find them easy out of the box, but don't feel you have to master everything at once. It's a useful application from the very first document! And, I loved being able to get a full featured download and create a half-dozen usable forms for a remarkably moderate price.

Pathagoras is a solid, "meat and potato", daily benefit to your practice, your staff, and your clients right out of the Box.

And, I am not a Robot. You can find me in Buckhannon, WV, pop. 6000.

11.   Brand New WV Custody and Alimony Law

Note to my readers: I apologize for the limited nature of this post, but it is the end of a long week, and I need time to digest these major revisions to West Virginia's Child Custody and Alimony Laws. This is a first impression.

I am told that Senate Bill 51, which you can Google, has been signed into law. I don't know when it goes into effect.

I reserve personal judgment on this law, which will impact the majority of my work days so long as it is in effect.

The revisions are to WV Code Article 46, Chapter 6, Section 301, and 48-9-205 and 48-9-206.

Things I notice immediately: I do not see "inequitable conduct" as a ground for increasing or decreasing the amount of alimony. There are 18 other factors which seem to be the old ones, length of marriage, incomes of the parties, health of the parties, age of the parties, etc. But, Para. 20 allows the court to consider, "..any other factors the court determines necessary or appropriate to consider in order to arrive at a fair and equitable grant of spousal support and separate maintenance."

That seems to leave the door open to a court who deems infidelity or spouse beating to be "necessary or appropriate to consider".

On the custody side, I consider this to be a big win for the "men's rights movement". The requirement that the court consider the apportionment of "caretaking functions" performed by the parents or third parties (grandparents, day care, etc.) prior to separation is gone, as is the provision that temporary arrangements entered into after separation but before suit is filed cannot be considered by the court. Now, apparently they can.

It does seem to elevate "best interests of the child", which seems like a good thing, but my guess is, "the devil is in the details".

This law evaded my radar even though I am on the WV State Bar Board of Governors, the Family Law Committee, the Family Court Mediation Subcommittee, the Future of the Law: Technology Committee and The WV Association for Justice Board of Governors.

I did track two prior bills; one I labeled the "One Size Fits All and the Children Can Go to Hell" bill; the other was the one that favored, "the parent best able to involve the other parent in the life of the child".

I tried to paste the urls of those articles here, but the full preview of the site appeared. So, just go to www.hunterlawfirm.net hit the tab to search my blog and enter "custody"; you will find 67 articles including the two listed above, plus "The Maze of Child Custody in WV", which will now have to be revised. (Drats!), and my "Winning Your Child Custody Case" and "Winning Your Custody Case II". The last two define "winning" as involving the other parent and learning to co-parent as the definition of "winning".

This new law has that language about involving the other parent, so something has been in the works for at least the last 2-3 legislative-sessions.

Any lawyer who has paraded family, friends, teachers, doctors, neighbors, and hired shills (no I never hired any), to lie (I mean testify) to the incredible, sensitive, attentive, and competent parenting skills of their client, won't miss day-long hearings on the percentage of caretaking functions testimony.

But, since the history of parenting still has relevance, it may be wishful thinking that we can avoid those days.

I think that the ability of parents, primarily mothers, to move to another state with the children will be impaired because I did not see the former provision granting a "presumption" to a parent who already was awarded "the substantial majority of caretaking", which was defined as 70% or more of the child's overnight time. This could have a huge adverse impact on women.

It seems like an artificial standard, as are the rules of baseball. But, giving that parent the presumption, and denying it to parents with less than 70% provided some predictability which may soon be lost.

I am going to post this quickly and copy it to one of the co-sponsors and authors of the bill and see what he has to say. I have removed his name from above and will attribute only if he says it is ok. I believe he worked hard to moderate the bill which might have had "Draconian" impact on WV child custody.

But, as a guy who represents mothers and fathers, my simple preliminary conclusion is that the old law was not perfect, but it did tend to favor the nurturing "hands-on parent", and value those hands-on moments better than "bringing home the bacon", protecting the house from intruders, and playing with the kids when it was convenient.

So, over the last 40 years, we went from ther "presumption" in favor of mothers, to the "primary caretaker rule", which also favored mothers more often than not, to a consideration of "caretaking functions" during the two years prior to separation, which also tended to favor mothers, to this new version which I believe will be used by its proponents to say that the default should be co-equal, 50% – 50% caretaking. If that's the law, so be it.

I will play that card for my male clients if they truly believe 50% – 50% is best for their child and are committed to being a caretaker. (Caveat: remember, "Be careful what you ask for.; you just might get it!")And I will fight like the dickens for what we used to call "the 90% mother", staying at home, loving, conscientious, and devoted.

Most of all, I hope that the best interests of the children will be the top priority. My biggest worry is that this will become known as the, "Girlfriends and Paternal Grandmother Custody Law."

They say, "If it ain't broke, don't fix it." I wonder if that maxim will apply to this new law. I suspect it will have ramifications way beyond what I can tell from three quick readings of this law.

I am also told a formula of sorts, like the one used for child support, will be used in the future to calculate alimony. That's is something that has long been needed.

I will update this as information becomes available.

12. Stupid Lawyer Trick #27 – The Trigger Happy Contempt Petition

I am painfully aware that I come across with posts like this as an arrogant "know-it-all". Do you think I like that? I hate it! I write these things in spite of wanting to be nice and constructive, not because I want to hurt feelings or offend. I do want to share ideas that will help our profession.

"Number 27" is just another set of suggestions that I think can help us be better lawyers.

First, a generalization. I have found that some lawyers build a reputation partially connected to the size of their retainers. People assume, since it works for dishwashing liquid and cookies, that "You get what you pay for."

For me, the factors of conscience, compassion, and commitment to clients' well-being must balance the drive to become wealthy and famous. When I come home, if my wife knows I did my best and did something for someone a competitor might not have, that's worth more than money. Don't get me wrong, money is important. I like money. But the client must come first.

Yet, I find the lawyer with $7500-$10,000 in her/his trust account is simply not as interested in getting to the bargaining table as I am. Being from a small town, most of my clients run out of funds before that, so I have worked hard on the "affordability" issue, and "access to justice".

I think that giving partial refunds, cheerfully and timely, helps one's reputation, and helps balance criticisms for being "too pushy". And, a world of credit cards has made billing somewhat easier.

But let me get to the specific criticism I have of some lawyers. It galls me to be hired by a client who has been sued for contempt and to learn that the opposing lawyer never wrote, called, or complained to my client even once.

I addressed this and other issues in "So You Have Your (Child Custody) Agreement – Now What?" http://hunterlawfirm.net/so-you-have-your-child-custody-agreement-now-what/.

I wrote "Now What" for clients who achieve an agreement but don't know how to enforce it or make it work. I was prompted to do so after a good agreement failed a young mother who had to hire me, and I learned that a colleague who is an excellent lawyer had neglected to instruct the client on what to do if the other person violated it, or the situation changed. I realized I hadn't been either!

So, now every client of mine who reaches a parenting agreement receives, and must promise to read, that article and two others: a. "THE SECRETS TO 'WINNING' CUSTODY OF YOUR CHILD", http://hunterlawfirm.net/the-secrets-to-winning-custody-of-your-child/ and, b. "THE SECRETS OF WINNING, Number II" http://hunterlawfirm.net/the-secrets-of-winning-number-ii/ These "how to" articles teach how to involve the other party in the life of the child while looking good for doing it.

It occurs to me that I need also to do a piece, "So You have Your Property Settlement Agreement, Now What?". Be sure to subscribe to this blog, so you will get it as I hit "publish".

In the two contempt cases I talked about, the persons who later hired me had misunderstood their agreements and inadvertently violated them. A good letter or two, or even three, citing chapter and verse of the Property Settlement Agreement or Final Divorce Decree could have avoided the litigation.

BUT, such letters might also cost the lawyer that big fee! Hmmm?

Ironically, an e-mail reminder, a text, a letter, certified letter, or ominous warning notice not only can often move the offending party out of their lethargy, but it is great documentation of the contemptuous attitude we are alleging. If you are filing a contempt petition, that's good stuff to have in your file.

Here is the advice I once got in a seminar from brilliant lawyer and friend Jim Bordas, "Give them the opportunity to do what's right, and be ready to punish them if they do wrong."

That's a good motto, and remember, "Do unto others as you would have others do unto you."

The lawyers who lack imagination, or who put earning that fee above the best interests of the client, fall short of the standards to which we should aspire.

Put the interests of the client first, and you will always have plenty of clients.

13. WV's Child Custody Relocation Statute: A Critical Issue for Parents and Children

I met with a new client recently because she had encountered an obstacle to her plan to relocate the parents' two-year-old child several states away. The father had objected to the mother's notice of relocation. I was surprised when she said that my blog had only an oblique reference to "relocation of a child". So, here is a "quick fix" and my serious warning:

A.   The good news for the parent who objects to their child moving away, you now have a fighting chance. The good news for the parent who desires to move is that you can make a reasonable prediction of the eventual outcome if you do your homework.

B.   The WV Relocation Statute, WV Code 48-9-403, is rather straightforward, but it has significant potential pitfalls for the parent on each side of this serious issue. Here's the link: https://tinyurl.com/ycvtvb7q .

C.   The key question is whether the proposed move will "significantly impair" the other parent's rights under the current court ordered parenting plan. You probably should stop for a moment and read the statute cited above. If you are in my blog, just click the hyperlink, but please return.

D.   When I began my practice, motions to relocate with the child were routinely granted to "the primary caretaker". I will not recite the history here, but until recently, the moving parent could still expect to take the child to the new home if she had been awarded "the substantial majority", of parenting time, that is 70% of overnight time.

E.   "The 70% rule" allowed a parent, usually the mother, to have a legal "presumption" in favor of the move so long as it was in good faith for a legitimate purpose. The statute lists examples. If the move is for something other than one or more of the causes listed, the presumption in favor of permitting the move disappears, and "best interests of the child" becomes the standard, as it is if the moving parent does not have the "substantial majority of parenting time".

F.   If you file the notice, and the other parent does not object, you can expect to be able to move, but you will need to renegotiate a parenting plan. If you file your own notice, using common sense, and the other parent objects, you are likely to learn your notice is inadequate.

G.   As I reread the statute today, I am reminded that it is nuanced. You should read it out loud, word for word, with the attorney, and apply it to your situation. Failure to do so can have dire consequences.

H.   I wrote about WV's new child custody law back in April: http://hunterlawfirm.net/brand-new-wv-custody-alimony-law/ . This law does not revoke or modify the relocation statute, but I noted then that in removing the "caretaking functions" history as a major component in determining residential care (custody), the legislature appears to be swinging the pendulum in the direction of the fathers.

I.   I have anecdotal information that it is becoming harder for the traditional "primary residential parent" to be able to pick up and move with the child. I expect to see an increasing number of contested proposed moves.

J.   So, my best advice is either retain record counsel and file a notice of relocation and petition to modify custody at the same time or consider finding a "legal coach" or consultant to assist you in preparing you notice. This is a time when using this option of "unbundled legal services" may be a good option, or perhaps it is your only option if you are short of funds. For more on "unbundling", just type "unbundled" into my blog's search engine. www.hunterlawfirm.net/blog/

K.   I believe the time that the custodial parent could simply file the notice of relocation and expect to be permitted to move the child has passed and that these moves should be carefully planned and notices of relocation carefully worded.

IV.
CONTINGENCY FEE CASES AND CLAIMS

1. If I Could Know Only Ten Critical Things About My Serious Injury Claim, What Would They Be?

This is as simple as I can make it.

A.   Unless you or someone very close to you has been through a serious injury, claim, and suit, what you think you know is not accurate. Preconceptions are killers.

B.   The percentage of really good personal injury lawyers is the same as dog catchers, @ 10%.

C.   A good injury lawyer is not an ambulance chaser. He or she cares about you and your family, but he isn't "Mother Theresa". He cares about getting ahead and making a living too.

D.   The entire system is based on the question of whether a person or company violated a duty (is "at fault") and seriously injured you or yours.

E.   The key to the system is INSURANCE which almost no one understands.

F.   Coverage in your own insurance policy, uninsured coverage, underinsured, a personal umbrella, or your medical plan, may make the difference between security and financial ruin.

G. Good lawyers avoid trials, but they have three key skills;

    i.   Ability to create a system for gathering information, and thus, a well trained, efficient, staff and modern office;

    ii.   Negotiating ability;

    iii.   The ability to try your case if it does not settle.

H. Different injuries may require different attorneys. Auto accidents, truck collisions, industrial disasters, product liability, falls on commercial property, insurance bad faith, and medical or legal malpractice have different ground rules. It is best to find someone who knows the difference and can bring in other attorneys or experts if needed.

I. The lawyer with the catchiest, or funniest, television ad may NOT be the lawyer most respected by his peers.

J. You can learn about the lawyer who authored this little post at, www.hunterlawfirm.net , or under the name "J. Burton Hunter III" on Facebook, Twitter, LinkedIn, or Google Maps, and if you e-mail him at hunterjb@hunterlawfirm.net and ask politely, he will send you a PDF file of his 1200 page book.

2. 29 Simple Facts About Your Personal Injury Claim

Starting with Ronald Reagan, and later Carl Rove, common perceptions of our civil justice system have hardened in to negativity, even against victims. But here are some real, simple, facts:

Good lawyers will always "push the envelope," so some personal injury claims will be marginal. That's life and human nature. Good judges can deal with them.

Our system of personal injury liability, such as auto, truck, and motorcycle collisions, premises liability, and dangerous products are based on your and my standards of right and wrong, the ones we grew up with.

The concept is "duty." I have a duty to pay attention, to refrain from texting while driving, to drive with enough rest, and to drive without intoxicating substances in my body. I have a duty not to injure you or yours.

In other words, we all have the duty to follow "The rules of the road."

The State of WV follows a concept called "comparative fault."

In WV, a personal injury claimant may only recover if her or his mistake is less than yours. If hers is 51 % and yours 49 %, as determined by the fact-finder, she bears her own loss. A claimant who is 20 % at fault may recover only 80 % of his damages.

So, most settlements and awards go to people who are primarily not at fault. With proper representation, the system works.

The measure of "compensable damages" is fairly easy to calculate. I leave the concept of punitive, or punishment, damages for another day.

Damages cover several elements:

Physical trauma, injuries;

Reasonable medical bills, past and future;

Lost Wages, past and future;

Temporary and permanent impairment, or what some call "disability;"

Past and present "pain and suffering;"

Mental anguish, "psychic pain." This includes post traumatic, cognitive, and emotional injuries;

Past and present loss of enjoyment of the benefits and pleasures of life;

Disfigurement, scars, deformed bodies, or loss of limbs.

These damages are both "economic" and "non-economic" loss. Legislatures often try to limit, or cap, non- economic loss for some types of tort claims such as medical malpractice. I do not discuss such claims here. And they protect some industries, such as negligent ski-resort owners, or gun manufacturers. Again, I am not talking of those cases here.

Lawyers who advertise heavily on television may be excellent, or maybe not. You may have them directly involved in your case; perhaps not.

75 % of "bread and butter" personal injury cases settle without suit, and 90 % settle without a trial. Why?

When fault is clear and injuries unambiguous, an experienced adjustor can reach compromise.

Where not so clear, a good lawyer may convince the carrier to go to pre-litigation mediation. Mediation often leads to settlement.

I have learned that I can make good money in cases with clear fault and "manageable" damages by taking a contingency fee of just 20 %, and occasionally less.

"Contingent" means no fee without a recovery. Many lawyers accept as standard 1/3, or 33 1/3 % of any sum collected, before costs are deducted, plus the costs. Many times, considering risk and delay, that is fair.

Personally, I don't think 1/3 is fair in routine cases where suit isn't filed. A 25 % fee is fine if I have to visit and photograph the scene, hire a reconstructionist, or make the case for fault. But if the carrier spares me that effort, 20 % is ok for clear fault cases. That's my opinion, and it works.

Some contingent fee cases justify 36 % to 40 %. Think major products liability, such as an exploding tire, medical malpractice, with its huge litigation costs, or industrial accidents, exploding mine or gas well, with expert engineers and complexity. I am not talking of them here.

Back to the reasons cases settle: with $50,000 in per person liability coverage and $40,000 in medical bills, or where injuries are permanent, that case is going to settle.

In those cases, would you rather pay $ $16,666.67 in lawyers' fee, (1/3) or $10,000,, (1/5) $7000, or even less. Don't expect the TV ad guy to cover his advertising costs and give you that break.

An experienced personal injury trial attorney can handle most traffic collisions just fine, and he/she can curate cases, identify the larger value or more complex cases, and associate with a top flight state-wide firm when needed.

My goal in this article was to make personal injury cases easier to understand, but not so clear that you think, "I can handle that."

Adjustors have done hundreds or thousands of cases. They know your case's value. Find someone who knows how to deal with them, and trust them with your future. Good luck!

3.   25 Personal Injury Related Definitions

These are not "legal definitions," nor is this legal advice, but it may come in very handy for you.

A.   **Negligence:** a simple mistake. Travelling too fast, rolling through a stop sign, mistakenly turning head on into a "one way" street.

B.   **Tort:** an injury one person does to another, sometimes as the result of negligence or gross negligence, and sometimes intentional. All are actionable, subject to comments below.

C.   **Tortfeasor:** a person who or entity which commits a tort.

D.   **Comparative Fault:** in WV a person is barred from collecting damages from another party or entity if that person contributed to her/his fault by 50% or more. They are then limited in their complaint by the percentage of fault the other party committed. For example, if the claimant has 40% of the fault and a $100,000 claim, and the tortfeasor has 60%, his award should be $60,000.

E.   **Liability Coverage Limits:** the most common example is auto insurance, which has state mandated limits of $25,000 per person and $50,000 per occurrence. This means that an individual injured by a negligent insured driver can collect a maximum of $25,000, but 2, 3, or even 5 injured persons are capped at $50,000. When their claims are over $50,000, a court will have to determine the apportionment unless the parties can agree. Other coverages can be $100,000-$300,000, $200,000-$600,000, or even higher if you have a "personal umbrella."

F.   **Personal Umbrella:** Think of "umbrella insurance coverage" as coverage that hovers over your other coverages in order to provide an extra level of protection. A condition of coverage is for you to carry robust limits in your underlying (auto, homeowners') policies. In return, you can have an additional coverage of $1,000,000 or more. It is a great bargain for persons with assets to protect. For more information on such issues, search of my blog gets 18 "hits" for the term "umbrella,"
      http://hunterlawfirm.net/?s=umbrella.

G.   **Uninsured Motorist Coverage (U.M.):** is insurance protection for you in case the person who injures you has no liability insurance. In WV uninsured motorist coverage is mandatory in limits of at least $25,000 per person and $50,000 per occurrence.

H.   **Underinsured Motorist Coverage (U.I.M.):** is the same concept as "uninsured;" it permits you to file a claim, based on negligence and injury by "the other guy," against your own insurance, without being penalized. You can waive U.M. coverage over $25,000/$50,000 and all U.I.M. coverage. Occasionally, we can get you the state minimum coverage if your insurance company failed to get a signed waiver from you.

Important Note: If you are a person with sufficient assets to protect or large enough conscience to want to have a "personal umbrella," you should be make sure, in writing from your umbrella carrier that your umbrella is included in the limits of your UM and UIM coverages. Get this in writing; it can make the difference between financial security and financial disaster! A simp**le, yet important rule.**

I.   **"Medical Payments," "Family," or "Med-Pay" coverage:** This is coverage that pays for your or your passengers' medical bills regardless of fault. It can be $5000, $25,000, or even $100,000! It is primary before your personal medical insurance, so it is something you should surely consider having in most cases.

J.   **Subrogation Claim:** is a claim that your insurer has for reimbursement for payments made on your behalf for medical services or perhaps even for your paycheck. I think of "subrogation" as a synonym for "substitution" or "standing in your shoes." It reflects "common sense" that the tortfeasor, and not an "innocent" insurer. should pay your medical bills.

K. **Made Whole Rule:** WV has a "made whole rule" that requires the subrogated entity to accept its pro-rata share of any settlement or judgment. It can't collect its entire claim unless you are recovering your entire claim. Often a good attorney will negotiate the subrogation claim as part of the global negotiations, so the carrier and the client each get a fair proportion.

L. **The Employment Retiree Income Security Act (1974), "E.R.I.S.A":** is a federal law governing many retirement and medical insurance plans. In my experience, it can be even more difficult to negotiate with an E.R.I.S.A. plan representative than those of many other organizations. Similarly, that is also often the case with Workers' Compensation or military subrogation plans. Use caution and the help of a good lawyer.

M. **Wrongful Death Claim:** West Virginia's wrongful death statute allows recovery from an at fault "tortfeasor" for the death of a person. The claimants are beneficiaries defined by the statute, including dependent children, a spouse, parents, and certain other persons. Keys are the closeness of the relationship between the decedent and the survivor dependent, the income potential and life expectancy of the decedent, and the amount of pain and suffering the decedent endured.

N. **Punitive Damages: are not** tied to compensation such as lost wages, medical expenses, or impairment. There must be intentional or willful, wanton, and reckless behavior by the tortfeasor. Punitive Damages are designed to punish and deter future wrongdoing, particularly by a large entity. As in the "McDonald's Coffee Case," punitive damages may be affected by the assets of the tortfeasor. In that case the damages were based on a couple of days of McDonald's "coffee profits."

O. **First Party Bad Faith:** This is a claim by an insured against their own carrier for "bad faith settlement practices." The claimant does not have to establish malice, or intentional wrong in order to recover compensation, damages for "aggravation and inconvenience," and lawyers' fees. The claimant needs only to "substantially prevail" in the prosecution of their claim to recover these items. But, in order to get "punitive damages," the claimant must also prove "malice," which is a finding of intentional wrongdoing.

P. **Third Party Bad Faith:** is bad behavior by "the other guy's" carrier. This cause of action no longer exists in WV, as our legislature outlawed it. You are limited now to a complaint through the WV State Insurance commission and possible "slap on the corporate wrist" of the insurance carrier.

Q. **Contingent Fees:** personal injury litigation and claim processing can be very expensive; thus, the most common fee arrangement is a "contingent fee." These fees may range from 10% - 40%. No fee is taken unless there is a successful recovery.

R. **Litigation Costs:** These costs include filing fees, acquisition of records, depositions, experts, travel, etc. Cost can be huge and the cost of the litigation must be considered in the evaluation of any settlement or the prospects for any law suit.

S. **Mediation:** This is a form of "alternate dispute resolution." A search of my blog gets 92 "hits": http://hunterlawfirm.net/?s=mediation . Mediation is supposed to be "non-adversarial," but it can still be pretty intense. As a result, most people prefer experienced, innovative, and creative mediators, and most such mediators prefer to keep the disputants in separate rooms. Mediators are usually lawyers or retired judges but can be from other professions such as accounting or psychology or the ministry. The problem there of course is they are inclined to bring their own standards and values to mediation, not legal standards. That's the time you should bring a lawyer, but, alas, often that's when people don't have a lawyer and give up their legal rights accidently.

T. **Medical Malpractice:** WV law permits recovery from medical providers who negligently deviate from "the standard of care," with various strong limitations that have diminished medical malpractice claims in WV by ¾ in recent years.

U. **"Deliberate Intent Claims":** are claims against an employer for industrial accidents and injuries that result from egregious behavior ("deliberate intent") and clear violations of industry standards. These claims are over and above Workers' Compensation claims, which are paid regardless of fault, at carefully circumscribed rates and applicable standards.

V. **Social Security Disability, and S.S.I (means tested) Disability Claims:** are governed by federal law and do not depend on establishment of fault. They do require the claimant to be disabled from all forms of gainful employment available in the national economy.

W.   **"Whiplash":** this is a demeaning term used by those generally skeptical of hyper-flexion, hyper-extension injuries. The most common event causing "whiplash" is a rear end collision where the injured person's body is driven forward by the seat back and the head, at the end of a slender stalk known as the cervical spine, bends sharply backward before being slung violently forward. The injury is often to the "soft tissue" tendons and muscles that have microscopic or larger tears, and disks or bursa that can bulge or herniate with painful results as they put pressure on radiating nerves. Because such pain is invisible to an observer, insurance carriers often make a huge effort to discredit such claimants, and a relatively few claimants may exaggerate such claims. From my experience, such injuries often result in utter misery, while a good clean break of a bone heals relatively rapidly, and with little permanent damage.

X.   **Impairment or Disability:** Impairment is the percentage impact on functionality; disability is the application of that impairment to what the claimant is able to do by education, training, experience, and age. Evaluating impairment and disability requires medical experts, vocational experts, and forensic accountants. It is complicated stuff, but not "rocket science."

Y.   **Frivolous or Junk Lawsuit:** This term was defined and refined by President George W. Bush's "meme maker" Carl Rove. I sometimes thought that President Bush thought that every claim ever filed that would require an insurance company or large business institution such as GM to pay a claim was "frivolous" or "junk." Here is my blog search for frivolous: http://hunterlawfirm.net/?s=Frivolous

Folks, this is the tip of the iceberg in a complicated subject, but I hope it was some use to you.

Follow the links to the searches I have posted above or just go to my website, www.hunterlawfirm.net. I have written hundreds of articles over 8 years, all of which you can find with a simple "search." Please provide feedback or contact me with your questions.

4.   I Want to be Your Personal Injury Lawyer Because..?

Questions and Answers for the Person Injured by the Fault of Another.

A.   These are good cases. They have a beginning, a process, and often a predictable end.

B.   The potential client really needs me. He/she/they are often afraid, confused, and uncertain where to turn.

C.   The client does not need to pay a large retainer. The fee is "contingent" on the lawyer's getting results.

D.   The size of the fee is directly proportional to the size of the recovery.

E.   The fee percentage can vary, dependent on the size of the risk.

F. The injury can be physical, emotional, financial, or, often, a combination.

G. An innovative lawyer looks to maximize the net recovery by the client. For example:

H. A $100,000.00 recovery can take two years, with the lawyer taking fees of$33,000 to $40,000, costs of $25,000, and medical insurance company subrogation claims of $20,000, netting just $15,000 to the client. Or;

I. Or, an $80,000 recovery can take just six months, with a 20% fee, $1000 in expenses, and subrogation costs of $14,000, netting the client $50,000. Here the client gets more, and the lawyer gets less, but both are satisfied because they get it sooner.

J. An experienced lawyer, in a clear fault case;

   i.   Will focus on educating the insurance adjuster;

   ii. Will document the medical expenses and lost wages as they come in, providing the insurance adjuster facts she/he need to adjust the "reserve."

   iii. The "reserve" is the fund of money set aside by the actuary to settle the claim.

   iv. It makes no sense to hold this information for the end, shocking the poor adjuster, and making it difficult to explain to supervisors why the adjuster miscalculated how much money to set aside.

v.   This critical detail is overlooked by many, many lawyers.

vi.   A good lawyer will prepare a letter for the client's friends, relatives, colleagues, and associates, asking for letters that describe the client, before and after the collision.

vii.   These "lay witness letters" are often filled with love or insight. They describe energetic, productive, people, who have to struggle with pain and impairment after a serious injury.

viii. When done properly, the presentment of an array of lay witness letters allows the claimant to avoid looking like a whiner.

ix.   Friends and family can describe courageous efforts by your client to ignore pain and physical limitations, or to cope with mood and cognitive disorders.

x.   Clients don't like to bother friends or family, or to draw attention at work, but a determined lawyer with a pesky paralegal can collect 20 lay witness letters where a "fill in the forms" lawyer may get only five or skip it entirely.

K.   These things make a difference.

Do your homework to find the person who can make that difference.

5.   Personal Injury: One to Bookmark

Have you ever been struck from the side by a New York City garbage truck going 45 mph? I have. I was the right front seat passenger, and the truck came from the right as our driver failed to see the red light on the corner. Being from WV, we always expected the light to be overhead.

Strangely, as I was in the eye of the tornado, my glasses came off and landed in the foot well, and one tooth was loosened, but I was otherwise unscathed. My friends in the back weren't so lucky, but we all survived.

But, I learned what the horrendous impact of a serious crash felt and sounded like. Words can't describe it, but I'll never forget it, and it happened 50 years ago.

Your crash may be like mine, or you may break a leg, lose an eye, severe a limb, break a back, or suffer a brain injury, leaving you looking just fine but knowing you just are not the same and perhaps never will be.

Please refer to two of my blog articles for information on insurances and how to protect yourself from ruin. http://hunterlawfirm.net/various-insurance-coverages/; and http://hunterlawfirm.net/buy-a-1000000-umbrella/

So, it was a bad one and now you do not know what to do. You or your spouse is in the hospital. If he is a worker, his paycheck may stop. If a small business person, who will make or sell your product, or pay your employee?

Who do you call first? Will your own insurance carrier protect you? What if the other side's insurance adjustor won't call you back? What if the other guy had no or inadequate insurance?!

What if he's throwing the blame back at you. What if he did not get cited? What if you did!

Oh, my! That's just a fraction of the questions you will have. So, you have heard of me, that I am hands on and nearby, or maybe your will remember this book-marked article and you call me, 304 472-7477.

Here's what happens:

A.   My staff has a short checklist to get your basic information, what happened, where, and what is worrying you. Occasionally they are permitted to mention a range of fees or to make an appointment, or they just put me on the phone.

B.   Or, they send me an e-mail before moving to the next thing, and I try to get back to you within an hour.

C.   Serious personal injury matters cause an alarm to ring. There is usually a component of urgency, and my paralegal of 15 years will usually come on the phone to get more details.

D.   When you and I talk for the first time, I have lots of narrowly focused questions. In 5-15 minutes, I know if I am interested, and I hope I can help, so I begin to answer your questions.

E.   You do not have to scrape up the money for a retainer, because personal injuries are handled on a contingency fee. When the lawyer is skilled at selecting the right cases, he is probably going to make more per hour than he can with a guaranteed hourly fee, so you have his interest. It is no wonder that lawyers are competing on TV for your business. These are desirable cases.

F.   If you are in the hospital or laid up at home, we will come to see you!

G.   The keys we look for in deciding if we can do you some good are:

H.   Serious injury:

I.   An insured or solvent "tortfeasor." That means they have liability insurance, you have uninsured or underinsured insurance coverage, or it is a large entity such as Fed Ex or Walmart.

J.   A strong probability of fault by the other guy.

K.   When we meet, I will get more details:

L.   What did the other guy do wrong?

M.   If you did something wrong, was your fault as bad or worse than the other guy?

N.   Do you have a medical insurance plan or auto coverage called "medical payments" or "family coverage?" We call it "Med Pay." It pays for your bills, regardless of fault, up to its limit, usually $1000-$25,000. Med pay is your first line of defense. Use it first!

O.   Where did this happen?

P.   When did it happen?

Q.   Who investigated it?

R.   Did the officer assess fault? He can't assess liability, but his opinion matters.

S.   Personal Data:

      i.   Spouse?

      ii.   Children?

      iii.   Job?

      iv.   Able to work?

      v.   Immediate concerns, questions?

T.   Insurance coverages? Med Pay, Uninsured or Underinsured coverage, group medical plan from work, personal resources, and whether you have "Umbrella Coverage.

It is very important for us to help allay your fears, to try to cancel your erroneous preconceptions, to answer your questions, and to deal with immediate concerns.

The adjustor often tries to dictate your auto rental company and to apply an arbitrary rule such as one week of rental. Truth is the tortfeasor is responsible for all reasonable damages incurred as a result of their insured's mistake. Your lawyer can help make that clear to the adjustor.

If we hit it off, and you decide to entrust your claim(s); yours, your spouse's, and your children's, to us, we are off and running:

i.   We have you sign a contingent fee agreement, 20% for clear fault settled out of court, 25% if liability is contested but still settled out of court, 1/3 (33 1/3 %) if suit filed, and occasionally 40% (but these are usually the medical negligence or industrial accident cases).

ii.   We order a police collision report.

iii. We order your medical records and bills.

iv.   If there is any serious question of fault, we visit the scene with you and photograph it. Mr. Hunter is an amateur photographer and has been taking many of his own photos for 40 years. He knows just what he wants to highlight, to show the court or the jury.

v.   He writes to the adjustor, setting out his working theory of the case and asking for written confirmation of his representation.

vi.   His paralegal sets up a schedule, to suspense the ordered documents, to follow up with the client, and to keep the adjustor informed.

vii. And, this is important. Since the adjustor has to establish and maintain a "reserve fund" for each case, we send him each wave of new bills and records and send him a short narrative of the challenges and progress of our client. That way the reserve can be nudged up gently, perhaps 20 times. This is critical, as an adjustor who set an insufficient reserve is going to have a lot of explaining to do, so better to get the reserve up in increments.

viii.   When we see the symptoms have persisted and the client is suffering, we send out a request for "lay witness letters". These are letters from people who are usually close to our client: spouse, children, siblings, parents, close friends, and co-workers. It helps if they knew the client before the collision.

ix.   These "lay witnesses" can observe the claimant when she or he isn't aware they are. Often the letters are poignant and compelling.

x.   When the adjustor learns we can provide 10-15 witnesses to our client's suffering, struggles, and stoicism, I think it motivates him to settle without requiring us to sue.

xi.   Sometimes we encourage the client to ask their doctor about referral to a specialist. With something subtle, like a closed head injury, I consult colleagues who work with lots of such cases.

xii.   If the claim is large enough to challenge the resources of our office, I have the luxury of calling any of several of the best firms in the state to associate. The shared fee is often no more than the original agreed fee, and if it is larger, we had better have a reason.

xiii.   If we have trouble reaching a negotiated agreement, I will sometimes suggest pre-litigation mediation to the adjustor. That give the adjustor some cover while keeping costs down. I have received over $1 million in such pre-litigation settlement meetings.

xiv.   If we have no choice, we file suit. That results in more expense, and the client is not expected to pay those expenses unless we recover.

xv.   The trial process is a subject for another day.

Above all, the client must be kept informed and be involved. This is not a problem where you can hire me and have me call you two years later to give you your check. One client advised that she and her postman had to say goodbye and hug after we settled her father's case, because they knew they wouldn't be delivering and receiving mail every few days from Burt Hunter.

When the time for recovery has come, we attend to the subrogation claims and unpaid expenses, we look at the possibility of a "structured settlement." When it is an infant's settlement, we consider a structured settlement, or something called a special needs trust which can help a recipient avoid losing eligibility for means tested benefits.

Where a financial advisor is needed, we are happy to make a referral.

It is always a relief when these difficult matters conclude, but they are not; I repeat, are not, matters you can do by yourself.

So, stick the URL of this article into your "bookmarks." We hope you and yours never need it, but use or share it if you do.

6. The Chinese Curse: May You Have a Mild Closed Head Injury

"Mild Closed Head Injury." It sounds pretty benign, as does the classic "Chinese curse," *May you live in interesting times.*

But, what is a "mild closed head injury"? Sadly, it can be a life changing event leading to permanent impairment, job loss, fractured relationships, depression, and even suicide.

As I write this, Baltimore police officers have been arrested for the death of Freddie Grey. Lost in the hub-bub was the officer who was hit by a rock thrown by a rioter who was "unresponsive." The next day, the police spokesman was asked how the officer was, and the response was, "He was unconscious for a while, but he is conscience and doing much better."

We may never hear from him again. It is likely his diagnosis is "concussion syndrome" and mild closed head injury. We have been hearing a lot about the serious consequences for pro athletes who suffer repeated concussions on the field. That makes sense, several serious blows to the head so that "Iron Mike" Webster of the Pittsburgh Steelers eventually became totally incapacitated and died,

 http://en.wikipedia.org/wiki/Mike_Webster.

And, there is Teddy Bruschi,

 http://en.wikipedia.org/wiki/Tedy_Bruschi, and so many others.

But, what about a person who was in just one auto accident, perhaps a rear-ender without an apparent strong impact with a solid object? The truth is that a closed head injury can occur with no direct strong impact, as a head is whipped back and forth; thus "whiplash." At first there are headaches, nausea, confusion, short term memory loss, sleeplessness, nightmares, and anxiety.

"But he'll be OK, right?" Not necessarily, and perhaps not without expensive and sophisticated diagnosis and treatment.

Once, a client of mine took a glancing blow from a large object that fell off of a trailer. He awoke and was embarrassed to see a circle of heads above him. He apologized that he had been "standing in the wrong place," which he had not, and may even have declined medical treatment. The eventual monetary settlement took a long time and much work but, even with financial relief, he eventually took his own life, with a handgun.

Another client, upon receiving a large check, thanked us profusely, but voiced his opinion that it was the specialized treatment and evaluation we had obtained for him that had restored his life. Money was secondary to being relieved of the agony of short-term memory loss, lack of focus and concentration, and an unhappy and worried wife. This man had been a leader of men and a skilled worker. He kept his job, but his productivity dropped nearly in half. He was just happy to get back to "near normal." The level of professionalism of the firm I found to associate with was superlative.

These are the people who our former President George W. Bush called malingerers, and their claims "junk lawsuits." If you agree with him for this kind of injury, pray, pray, that you never get to learn how wrong you are. Living it is hell.

So, if you or a family member or friend is injured by the fault of another, and just cannot seem to bounce back, or better yet, before you get to that stage, talk to an experienced lawyer and let him or her help you put together a plan for legal, medical, and personal rejuvenation.

Remember, unless the other party has large insurance limits, or you have protected yourself with underinsured coverage and/or a "personal umbrella," there may be little or nothing to recover. Here is what I recently said about that: http://hunterlawfirm.net/what-you-do-not-know-about-insurance-and-social-security-can-hurt-you/

Do I do these cases by myself? Nope: these cases need $30,000 - $100,000 of out-of-pocket investment by the lawyers, and 30 years in the WVAJ (Trial Lawyers) has taught me which WV firms do the best for such clients. I associate with one of them, for no greater fee than if the clients hired only one firm. So, the client has the benefit of local and "big city" trial counsel, and a chance, for a fresh start and renewed life.

So, hope for an injury free future, but call if you need us.

7. A Claim Against Your Own (Fire) Insurance Company: Bad Faith

Let's look at another kind of injury, bad faith by your fire insurance company:

You have a major fire.

The adjustor is overburdened, distracted, or may not even care.

The checks are slow in arriving, and you think your place is a total loss, but the adjustor does not.

It turns out you have some "environmental issues," and your limited rental coverage is running out while your damaged house is moldering down around you.

Some lawyers will immediately file suit against your insurance company, embarrassing the adjustor, putting him on the defensive, and creating an enemy.

Now your fee will be at least 1/3, and your litigation expenses may be $10,000, or more, and your moldering house will molder for a year or two, making it unrepairable even if it really was.

Once your lawyer sizes up your situation, your cash flow, health, age, and tolerance for risk, he might counsel a different approach, taking an up-front contingent fee of 8% to 10%.

If suit must be filed, you get a credit for fees paid.

The lawyer can help you pester, document, argue, and negotiate with the field level adjustor, not a high paid lawyer billing hourly, who has no incentive to make the case go away quickly.

The news to your client and the adjustor is that if your position eventually prevails, even without a lawsuit, the company will probably pay your fee, and the client will get damages for "aggravation and inconvenience."

As a friend and colleague of mine counseled, "Give them the chance to do the right thing. If they don't, punish them."

A.   When they do, the damages remain "manageable" and the clients get to move on with their lives, and;

B.   When they do not, you have a solid "bad faith settlement practices claim" as defined by the famous "State Farm vs. Hayseeds, Inc." WV Supreme Court of Appeals case. You can file suit with a clean conscience, knowing you tried to save your client and the company that grief.

The keys to this approach are:

i.   A lawyer who has been representing "the little guy" for a long time, and understands what is important to him; and

ii.   A lawyer who is used to working on a tight budget, so he focuses on the "net to client," on limiting expenses, and on moving the case forward as quickly as possible.

These cases do not get big headlines, but they enhance lives, and benefit people who just want to get on with their lives.

You may have to do some homework, search a bit closer to home, read online reviews, and ask around to find the lawyer who places the interests of the client above his own.

8.   Slip and Fall – Premises Liability – Then and Now – Personal Injury

I have often written blog posts about the history of technology from the perspective of a lawyer who has practiced his craft from 1972 to today. Compared to that, these two examples are unremarkable. You won't be surprised, but we should all be amazed.

Yesterday the subject of voicemail came up. My client said she had transcripts of all her voicemail. I knew this was possible, but we were surprised when she showed us the messages, verbatim, left by my staff for her. Clients with iPhones can now send us both the audio-file and a transcript. This may be more useful in family court than civil court, but it is a good thing to remember.

A.   Today we met with another client who was seriously injured by slipping and falling at the entrance to a large discount retail store in the area. She had gone back and taken a few photos.

B.   I turn down most "slip and fall" cases. Juries, and therefore insurance adjusters, like to hold people accountable for their own falls. "Why didn't she look where she was going?"

C.   But, the existence of (nearly invisible) ice at an entrance, the busiest foot traffic area of the store, is usually a pretty good basis for a claim, especially if the claimant was wearing good, well-treaded, shoes, as she was.

D.   It is not the same standard for a private residence where the visitor is called a "licensee," a person who is presumptively there primarily for their own benefit.

E.   Therefore, a person injured at a friend or neighbor's home has a much more difficult standard to meet. And many homeowners do not have liability insurance.

F.   Business "invitees" are presumptively there because the store, or its company, invited them to be there. It is the store that controls the walkways, the store that has the resources, to keep the primary walkways clear.

G.   So, I asked my paralegal to find the store on Google Earth. "No problem".

H.   "What are the coordinates (longitude and latitude) of the entrance?"

I.   "I am not sure which entrance she used."

J.   "Hmmm..? Can't you use street view?"

K.   "I don't know." Click.

L.   Suddenly we descend from a quarter of a mile above the store to find ourselves staring at the store entrance!

M.   There is the newspaper vending machine that is also in our client's photograph. Zooming in, we can see a crack in the pavement where she fell. It is almost as if we had a drone!

N.   We get a wide-angle view, a close up to the left, and a close up to the right. I will still stop by and take my own photo, but what a great start to getting a clear photo of the injury scene.

O.   20 years ago, I spent $300-$400 on a detailed weather report for the 24-hour period leading up to my client's fall. We had minute by minute data on the drizzling rain the day before, the incoming cold front, the time, within a few moments, that the entrance surface froze, and the number of hours that the sidewalk remained unsalted, @ 18, before my client stepped on "black ice" and ruined her knee.

P.   Did others' fall? We don't know. Perhaps there were a dozen "near misses." I do know a jury decided that the county's largest employer had been asleep on the job, and that no one spread salt where it should have gone.

Q.   That's the kind of "responsibility" a WV jury can understand!

R.   It will probably cost us $500.00 to get the hourly data and narrative that we need from www.compuweather.com .

If favorable, it can make our case. And, if not, better to know in advance.

9.   What Should I Do Six Months After My Rear End Collision?

The question above is a good one, but a tad late. Let's discuss whether it is too late.

If you took a small sum and signed a release of your injury claim, that's it. It's over, regardless of whether you have continued symptoms or treatment.

If you have limited medical insurance, or did not know you had medical payments "med pay" coverage, and therefore decided to "gut it out," and have received little treatment in spite of lots of pain, it will be difficult to get back on track and document your claim, but you may be able to.

If you have not kept a diary of events such as missed work, missed vacations, inability to engage family and friends, and inability to perform usual activities, you have work ahead reconstructing that information. It is much better to record that stuff as it happens. But, I stress that it may not be too late.

If you have not retained competent counsel, you must do so immediately. The title of this article assumes you have not hired counsel and that time is running out.

But, (you ask) "I thought I had up to two years?" Correct, but your tortfeasor may have moved away or died. Eyewitnesses may become unavailable. The accident scene can change. The police officer's memory can fade.

There are so many reasons to set aside your preconceptions and talk to an honest, experienced, professional, personal injury attorney.

While I expect to be hired once you realize that my goal is not to sue someone, that decision is yours after we chat. I am used to keeping costs down, working on my relationship with the adjustor, gathering information (the puzzle pieces) and a standard, orderly, manner, and submitting a detailed, well organized, comprehensive demand package.

As I write this article, today I settled a clear fault case, $21,000 in medical damages, relatively minor scarring of a forehead, for $80,000 cash and a waiver of the non-fault insurance carrier's "subrogation claim."

What does that mean?

A.   It means instead of 1/3, my fee is just 1/5 of any sums received. That's $12,500 instead of $20,000, the "standard fee" of many lawyers in our area.

B.   It can be 1/4 if we first argue over liability.

C.   It may be 1/3 if a suit has to be filed.

D.   But, many cases can be resolved because fault is clear, and the insurance company ready to save legal fees and risk by paying a reasonable settlement.

E.   It also means that the client gets to keep over $60,000 of "cold cash," most of which is not taxable!

F.   When you factor in litigation costs, risk, delay, and higher contingent fees, that $80,000 settlement is as good as a verdict of $150,000 two years from now. The client gets to keep just as much, and gets it sooner.

Why did I ask the question in the title? Because, if you have a valid claim, and still have not settled or hired competent counsel, you probably still have time, but it is rapidly running out. Call me soon, or perhaps regret it for life.

Of course, if you or yours becomes injured, you know I am here and that I believe you should call and become informed.

Either way, do not assume "common sense" is the solution. You simply do not know how to document your claim or negotiate settlement. You have no clue how to gather "lay witness letters" or how to use them.

The insurance adjustor knows that you are adversaries. He or she may be a good person, but they are overworked, and they get no incentive for paying more than the absolute minimum. Only if you demonstrate that you can go to court and get a robust verdict are you likely to settle for "full settlement value." If the carrier thinks you will eventually take whatever it offers, you will not get its best offer.

Here's hoping you have not and will not be injured, but that you give us a call if you are.

V.
MEDIATION, NEGOTIATION, AND SETTLEMENT

1.   Alternate Dispute Resolution: Mediation - A Foot in Each Camp

Thoughts following my attendance at the WV Association for Justice 54th Annual Convention and Seminar: I love being a plaintiffs' trial lawyer. By definition, we represent individuals. They are often facing one of the more trying times in their lives and are up against someone or something more powerful and wealthy than they. It is a terrific feeling to level the playing field and help someone achieve a just result (or just "to win!").

Small firms and sole practitioners sometimes lose their focus and feel they are the only ones fighting the good fight. Many, of course, are not passionate about what they do. The work is just a job. They long for eight hours a day, a steady paycheck and benefits, and a job without stress.

I love the thought of less stress, but have dealt with it for 40 years and see no way to eliminate it. I have learned to lessen it. The tips and techniques I discover and pass on allow for greater productivity and more enjoyment in the task. Solving a task and moving on to another is the story of my life.

My attendance each year at the WVAJ annual meeting recharges my batteries and reminds me that many WV lawyer seek excellence.

Simply sitting for two days and listening to some of the best in the business talk about what they have learned and how they apply it reminds me that I am not the only "smart guy" out there. WV has hundreds of very sharp, very dedicated lawyers, men and women. The best come at it with fire and passion, and it is contagious.

I have been writing a lot about efficiency, collegiality, mediation, and negotiations. I have also written about disingenuous lawyers and maddeningly inefficient judges. (Recently I sat for 2 1/4 hours as one of at least four cases the Court set for 9:00 a.m. How arrogant to cause 8-10 litigants to pay their lawyers up to $1000 extra dollars for 'the convenience of the Court'!)

Two very fine lawyers, Jamie Bordas (son of my friends Jim and Linda Bordas) of Wheeling and Gary C. Johnson of Pikeville, Ky. spoke on settlement negotiations and trial preparation and voiced opinions that appear to be contrary to my writings. After some pondering, I do not think they are.

Jamie challenged the old truism that the best mediated agreement is probably one where both sides are somewhat unhappy with it. He believes the best one is where we leave the room, clench our fist, and say "YES!"

Those of you who have read how frustrated I get at lawyers who obfuscate, prevaricate, and simply use dirty tactics will wonder how I reacted to Gary when he says, "Let them. I do not care. It runs off of me like water off a duck's back. It just makes me feel better when I beat them." Now there's a fellow I want to emulate.

Jamie told two excellent anecdotes:

1. His class team assignment, while a student at Notre Dame, was with classmate Jerome Bettis. Yes, that Jerome. The one all Steelers' fans love. They negotiated to a standstill

for four hours, being the only members of the class who failed to reach agreement, only to learn that they were the only ones who passed the challenge. The dispute was one that could not be negotiated with fairness to both parties. Those who gave in let their client be short-changed. What a great teaching too. I have learned some of my best lessens from my mistakes.

2. Jamie's college avocation was selling and trading tickets to Notre Dame football games. He was shrewd enough to select one type of buyer. The guy in the nice car with a pretty girl at his side. According to Jamie, "Those guys were NOT going to fail to get that girl into that game." So, of course, they paid the highest prices because Jamie knew they "wanted it too bad." I pondered the double meaning of "it."

Jamie and Gary, of course, have warrior mentalities. But, I stress that while each counseled us to negotiate tough and prepare well, neither suggested we resort to unethical or questionable behavior. But, trust me, if they were hockey players, it would not be a polite form of hockey.

Both reminded the audience that our adversaries do not care about the harm their client has done to ours. They do not want to make us feel better. They want to win, to save money for their clients, to feed their families, and to do well in their profession. I have heard such words from my wife Nancy, who understands human nature and reminds me to keep my guard up.

Please understand something. I agree with them. I detest losing. I want my clients to get a great result. I want people to admire me as a lawyer and person. I have more of that abrasiveness that my friend Mike Aloi taught, in another session, that we should try to avoid. My tendency over the decades has been to push hard for my client's position, sometimes too hard. This tendency is one reason I have spent time thinking about collegiality and professionalism.

And you also need to know that Gary and Jamie have outstanding reputations, as do their firms, and they get the really good cases. Recently, I was on the other end of that scale. I had agreed to accept a minor role as "local counsel" with an "out-of-town counsel." Then this "lead counsel" dropped the ball and got himself fired, and I was verging on trying a case I could not win.

I was holding perhaps a pair of twos. I followed all of their tips, made sure I had good experts, and prepared as if we were going to trial. Eight hours of mediation got us a meager settlement, but it was a meager settlement in a case that never should have been filed. It was a great lesson; do not sign on as "local counsel" unless you are ready to take on the full responsibility of the case.

1. So "camp number one" in my title is Jamie's and Gary's world, of personal injury, malpractice, industrial injury, and insurance bad faith. The adversaries are wealthy and powerful, and the liability component is usually strong for plaintiff. AND, the issue is money, how much if any money?

2. But, look at the difference in "camp number two," family law mediation. The parties often were married. They certainly were intimate. They believed they loved one another. Usually they have produced a child or children together, and they built whatever estate they have together. The personal injury victim and the tortfeasor can walk away after the money changes hands and never see one another. Often these people cannot.

Divorcing parties or parties with children still have to raise those children. There are schooling decisions, discipline, medical treatment, graduations, failures, weddings, births, funerals. They have to learn NOT to ruin their children's lives by screwing up the divorce as badly as they did the marriage.

When we seek money for our PI clients, the more money the better! Everything we squeeze out of the other party in a family law case, diminishes the ability of that party to pay his bills, provide for his family, and live a secure existence.

I have seen people pull back from what I recommended or the court would give because they felt it was too great a burden on the other side. I like such people, although they can be frustrating.

And, if you "don't care" what dirty trick the other counsel does, are you really being true to your profession?

Should we not call out the other party on such silliness:

1. As the lawyer who claims not to know what a "significant other" is in a discovery response;

2. Or the one who is trying desperately to keep out an e-mail because he knows it is a smoking gun proving his client's infidelity (and she wants to be able to lie to the court about it);

3. Or the one who answers under oath that she has not identified any witnesses or potential exhibits two weeks before she discloses 24 witnesses and 100 exhibits?

I think we should, and I think judges should, penalize dirty players, which they will not do most of the time. To them it is just "petty squabbling by the lawyers." Sadly, they do not seem to expect high standards, and often they get what they expect.

I was raised to believe in right and wrong and believe in playing by the rules. In the heat of battle, have I done otherwise? I take the "fifth amendment."

Finally, the family law client usually has nothing like the resources available to them as the client with a contingency fee contract, where their lawyers may advance $20,000-$50,000 in funds and more than that in time. Those firms are prepared to spend six, even seven, figures in litigation expenses, with a prospect of a BIG contingent fee. There is risk of loss of course, but these guys and their firms often "win big."

I have put $10,000 of time into a case knowing I would never get paid. Once it was $30,000 (don't like to think about it) Those are the cases where the other side has pissed me off, or the client is very worthy, or my reputation is on the line. But, most of the time, costs MUST be considered in a family law case.

Still, it is nice to have a foot in each camp, and to remember that our clients need us to be warriors. It is also good to remember that our clients need us to understand people, and human nature, and to be able to take the long view. Will getting you the motorcycle really change your life over time?

I have been at mediations where we said at the end, "Yes!" I have been at others where we just said "Whew!" and even ones where we said something unprintable but took the deal anyway.

A good general trial lawyer maintains a proper balance between being a warrior and a pragmatist, as Jamie recommended when he reminded us not to let our egos get in the way of a fair settlement.

I will try to follow Gary's advice and allow the bad behavior to roll off my back and to have the payback be my results. That was very good advice.

2.   Keys to a Successful Mediation

FUNDAMENTALS OF MEDIATION

I sometimes forget how little the average litigant, and even judges, know about mediation. There are no riveting serial television dramas staring a team of courageous mediators. Although my wife loves "Bull" a dramatic series about a courageous and brainy jury consultant.

By rule, judges may not even be told what goes on in mediation, so here are some insights for them and you. I mediated a case successfully yesterday, but I made a rookie mistake. I thought I got an offer to take to the other side, but they were holding back, and I missed it. That faux pas set us back but did not derail the mediation.

When I went back to that side believing we were only $9000 apart, we were really $15,000 apart. I had misunderstood the first side's settlement position. That was embarrassing, and it was harder to get to the compromise number. I also showed the famous "Burt Hunter pique'," and that's not a good thing. We live and learn.

However, I kept one principle in mind, and that led to the settlement, always try to reduce the number of disputed issues. It was a divorce division of property and debt mediation. We started with twenty variables, but one attorney had produced an outline that allowed the parties to stipulate to ownership and values of more than half of them.

We worked hard for an hour or so on various values, and the BIG issue, whether three of the assets were partially or all marital assets, or separate. Separate assets are ones a party owned before the marriage, had received by gift or inheritance from someone outside of the marriage, or was separate because it was a personal injury settlement.

Another key to this successful mediation is the lawyers remained engaged, cordial, and collaborative throughout the negotiation. And, one lawyer had a "hard stop" requiring his attention, so negotiations got serious an hour or two earlier than they might have. That's probably a good reason not to leave a whole day for a routine mediation. We tend to fill the time we have available. But the lawyer and party who do not have a "hard stop" keep options open.

When we got down to 3-4 variables, I suggested the other side turn it into a cash demand for "equalization" of the equitable distribution. That means that even though the parties did not agree what the family residence was worth, how much of the equity one of the parties had a claim to, and what the reconstructed vintage automobile was worth, we had reduced the dispute to one issue, money.

When we got to two numbers that were close enough that it would cost the parties more to litigate the issue than to compromise it, we were almost there. It wasn't close enough to "split the difference" but almost.

One party used a technique that could have derailed our efforts but was smart enough to abandon it when necessary. My recollection is I learned that technique from "Getting to Yes – Negotiating Agreement Without Giving In" by William L. Ury. I read it the first time in the late '80's. That technique, as I remember it, is to have a beginning offer, a fallback number, and a bottom line. That won't work in Family Law negotiating for two reasons:

A.   Sometimes there are 20-30 issues, so offers must be innovative and fluid; and,

B.   For at least a decade, I kept coming back from mediation having accepted less than my "bottom line" and I could not figure out why.

I eventually learned why from WVU College of Law Professor Tom Patrick who showed us a graphic similar to the one below. The curves at the outer edges of the page are each party's starting position, the second line is the fallback, and the third is their "bottom line." As I explain to my client, it is the circle in the middle that contains the tough territory, the place neither party wants to go.

But, in most instances, each party must go somewhere inside that circle to reach agreement. It might be dead center, but it might be closer to one party's "fallback position" if that is the more reasonable position.

Each party might not be starting from a reasonable position. Sometimes my client's real desire is so close to the likely result that we must create an illusory first demand to get there. No one likes to think he or she must meet the first demand of the other party. Bad negotiators arrive, state their position, and never move from that position throughout the day. Such mediations are doomed to failure.

I go into mediation knowing my client's concerns and goals. I have talked about my information gathering techniques in a recent post:

http://hunterlawfirm.net/digging-2018-short-sweet/ .

My "regular mediators" sometime ask to look at "Mr. Hunter's top ten lists," knowing that I have had them make numbered lists of their worries, goals, and complaints about the other side. These lists are helpful in that they let me give the mediator and the judge concise summaries of the issues in the case and our positions. But I do not go into mediation with three pre-conceived offers in mind. The reason I don't is I do not know what the other side is going to say or reveal. Two examples:

i.   **I once went into a BIG personal injury mediation with a chip on my shoulder.** The other side, in a seven-figure case, dragged their feet so my clients could not get the original limited liability limits of $20,000 per person prior to Christmas, adversely impacting their, and my, holiday. (We were dealing with the underinsurance carrier at mediation).

The mediator, a friend, took me aside and cautioned me to tone it down (there's the famous 'Burt Hunter pique' again!) because the other side had found a letter from my client's doctor in his medical record which severely compromised his claim to have been in good shape before the collision. That letter probably cost us $200,000 which we had to concede to make the deal. Fortunately, but it was still a good settlement. Had I to do it over, I would have not started on a "high horse" because it was somewhat embarrassing to have to climb down from that horse.

ii.   **In another case, I fully intended to get my client $50,000 for a hip injury.** His hip had been "frozen" for 40 years from an infection related to tuberculosis when he was 13 years old. A side impact auto collision "unfroze" the hip, leaving rough joint surfaces to rub and become inflamed. Within 60 days he was required to retire from his trade as a barber. Before the planned mediation, I got a call from the other lawyer.

We had signed a release for him to get my client's social security records. During the initial Social Security exam, my client had, under oath, sworn that he had sustained "no serious injuries" during the five years before he filed his disability claim!

When I asked him "Why?!," he answered, "I thought if I told them the truth, they would deny my disability claim." Having established without doubt that my client would lie for money, we had no choice but to lower our demand.

Neither of these cases would have settled if we had rigidly stuck to our preconceived ideas.

My point is that until mediation begins it is hard to understand the other side's position, argument, and facts. I have come to mediation of one mind and left knowing that I would never have wanted the judge or jury to hear that case. More often, the compromise was predictable, but mediation is still necessary to get the clients to a position where they could settle.

Finally, a family court judge who had been a magistrate most of her career admitted to me, "I have never attended mediation."

Another judge bragged, "In my twenty-year career, I never went to mediation with my client." I respected the first judge, for her candor and for the fact she simply had never had the opportunity.

The second judge, not so much. She had just proudly admitted to sending her client to negotiate her own case! To me that is both malpractice and a wasted opportunity!

This is the common, if misguided, practice in other parts of the State. In North Central WV, we know negotiating is an acquired skill that requires study and practice to achieve.

Final tips: prepare and educate your client, listen, advocate, argue, but remain pragmatic and flexible, and most cases will settle!

(**Note:** I have received some constructive criticism that my effort to promote common mediation rules for all courts is an over-reach. I understand that criticism, and will try to address it. The rules for circuit and family courts are detailed, and the drafters have a proprietary interest in them. And, standards must be maintained, and methods in place for the payment of mediators. I would opt for ambiguity so that such things can get sorted out in the process, just like the Founders did when they moved from the Articles of Confederation to the U.S. Constitution.)

3.   Is It Time to Revise Mediation in WV?

But I still answer the mediation question above with a resounding "Yes!" Here are my thoughts:

A.   I first wrote of the history of mediation in WV all the way back in 2010:

B.   The limitation of family court mediation to "children's issues" was a terrible mistake. It led to some terrible deals and inhibited the implementation of mediation in family court and of lawyers' participation in the mediation process. Mediation should be for "children's issues," property division, debt division, alimony, everything. Special challenges when domestic violence and substance and alcohol abuse must be recognized and dealt with.

C.   And I elaborated on some of the differences between "civil mediation" and "family mediation" in 2012: http://hunterlawfirm.net/a-foot-in-each-camp/ .

D.   I also wrestled with the differences between juvenile abuse and neglect and family court: http://hunterlawfirm.net/children-guardians-ad-litem-the-law-and-society/ .

E.   And I really struggled to capture the myriad conflicts and overlaps of what is generally called "custody": http://hunterlawfirm.net/the-maze-of-wv-child-custody-issues-just-dropping-crumbs-wont-get-you-out/

F.   But that's exactly my point. Differences in courts, and the assumptions under which the courts operate, make detailed mediation rules, and technical barriers to mediation, unworkable.

G.   One exception is criminal court, as I cannot foresee a way for mediation to be an aid to plea bargaining. But,

133

prosecutors and defense counsel would do well to master negotiation and communication techniques that mediators and counsel use in effectively resolving their cases.

H.   So, also, is a mental hygiene commitment hearing a good venue for mediation.

I.   As for the impediments to passing a new law, last year I worked with several others, including lawyer Tom O'Neill and State Senator Charles Trump, in obtaining passage of "The Family Court Restraining Order Law," WV Code Sec. 51-5A-5a. These orders prohibiting bad behavior that falls short of being domestic violence are being entered dozens of times a week all over the state. We kept the statute simple, and it seems to be working. I believe that passage of a new mediation law will also benefit WV families and litigants!

J.   Lawyers, Judges, Mediators, and Legislators need creativity and innovation to speed up our courts and expand justice to a greater number. Justice delayed, and justice that only a few can afford, are NOT justice.

K.   Last week, I glanced over the "rules of mediation" in each court and decided that you would not want a detailed description of them. Suffice it to say I think the rules are too technical and picky.

L.   And the "screening" provisions for family court do nothing but discourage mediation and foolishly try to predict which cases can be settled and which cannot.

M.   The default expectation should be that parties go to mediation, unless, upon proper motion, a party convinces the court it will be dangerous or endanger their health. If there are security concerns, the courts should have discretion to deal with that.

N.   I say that "the default" should be that parties to litigation should be expected to go to mediation and to participate in good faith.

O.   When I say "all parties," I mean the parties to civil suits in circuit courts, in magistrate courts (subject to funding and the ability of parties to pay, as this is "small claims court"), family court, and to fiduciary and guardianship hearings.

P.   And, to the extent there are non-party "players" such as grand-parents, interested persons, step-parents, etc., let them come mediate, but only if the parties agree. The more that "the players" can participate in negotiations, the better the chance the settlement will "take."

Q.   Persons subject to mediation should be given a brochure explaining mediation in some detail, including, for self-represented litigants, an explanation that they should come to mediation with an open mind, prepared to be flexible, and to put children first <u>when children are involved</u>. I stress "when children are involved," as my critic points out that suits arising from a rear end collision or medical malpractice do not involve the children. I think people are smart enough to figure out what "When children are involved." means.

R.   They should be reminded that this is their chance to fashion a monetary settlement, settle a law suit, parenting plan, or property settlement agreement by themselves, without technical rules of evidence, or time constrained hearings. People can fashion settlements that no court can order which are tailored to their needs and wants, while the court, acting on conflicting information, is unlikely to come up with anything better for them, their families, or their children.

S.   Here is an informal summary of my suggestions for the new mediation law or rule, which will be similar for all courts, magistrate, family, circuit, and business.

    i.   Whereas, as the alternate dispute mechanism called mediation has evolved and matured in WV.

    ii.   Whereas the rules for mediation are different, or non-existent, in various courts;

    iii.   Whereas, it is important, for the full realization of the benefits of mediation, that mediation be considered for every case, (except criminal and mental hygiene involuntary commitment proceedings), and that referral to mediation should be the default option, with opting out being granted only for good cause shown.

    iv.   The parties should confer early and determine if they can agree on a mediator and at least one alternate.

    v.   Represented parties should have their counsel present at this critical stage of the proceedings.

vi.   No mediator will be permitted to mediate in WV Courts if they object to the presence of a party's lawyer at mediation. They and the lawyers must learn to collaborate and cooperate. Civility is expected.

vii.   Lawyers admitted to practice in each court are expected to have obtained necessary training to meet the standards that have been established by the WV Supreme Court of Appeals.

viii.   Lawyers may opt in or out of the sliding fee scale of the WV Supreme Court of Appeals, but will be bound by the Supreme Court's fee Rules if they opt in. They will not be part of the referral rotation of the court if they have opted out of the sliding scale if the court, such as family court, utilizes it, but parties may still use such lawyers by mutual agreement.

ix.   Where public funds are not available, mediation is still the default unless the court permits "opting out" for financial hardship.

x.   Parties will not be required to meet face to face unless both parties and the mediator concurs. Caucusing is encouraged, and participation by phone is permitted if agreed to by all parties and the mediator.

xi.   Represented parties who sign a mediated agreement or parenting plan will be bound to the terms of the plan under the law of contract.

xii.   Unrepresented parties will be expected to keep their word and be bound by their signed mediated agreement unless there is a serious mistake of material fact or law. It will be discretionary with the Court whether to impose the agreement signed by an unrepresented party or parties.

xiii.   Non-parties such as family members, mediators in training, or interns will not be present at mediation without advance notice and agreement. The court may, upon proper motion, permit such a person to accompany the litigant.

xiv.   The Court may include appropriate provisions to assure security, such as requiring mediation to be at the courthouse, or even to require parties to arrange for private security, or by ordering mediation via conference call or FaceTime or Skype, or their equivalent.

xv.   Commissioners, such as fiduciary or mental hygiene, will administer these mediation rules as the courts do, with the same discretionary powers, subject to the jurisdiction of the court under which they operate.

xvi.   Parties are encouraged to utilize other alternative dispute mechanisms such as arbitration or "med-arb" so long as all parties agree and so long as the mechanism is stipulated to in writing.

xvii. The confidentiality of the mediation will be preserved, although mediators are obligated to inform the court if a party fails to appear, fails to pay timely, acts in a disruptive manner, or fails to mediate in good faith.

xviii. The person attending mediation must have "full settlement authority." When that person is an insurance adjustor, they will have the power to authorize settlement for the full demand or limits of coverage, unless stipulated otherwise by all parties and the mediator in writing.

xix. Violations may be enforced by the full contempt powers of the court.

In summary, I believe that if these mediation rules are implemented the efficiency, effectiveness, and justice of our courts will be measurably improved.

4. Family Court Mediation Streamlined – Some Ideas

Author's note: These ideas are mine. I have presented them to the WV State Bar Family Law Mediation Subcommittee and hope they will contribute to some positive change for WV families, and especially children and low-income litigants.

MEMORANDUM IN SUPPORT OF A CHANGE IN THE FAMILY COURT MEDIATION RULES

Before we try to rewrite the mediation rules, I would like to state the case in favor of a revision.

Our system sets up Litigants in divorce, custody, contempt, and modification cases as "adversaries."

These cases are often highly charged with emotion, are emotionally and financially draining, and they can drag on for over a year!

At the end, the parties often truly detest one another, and their children have suffered, only to have a court issue a ruling that isn't tailored to the parties' needs and may be something both sides dislike. It borders on "one size fits all" justice.

Something like 70% of family court litigants are not represented by a lawyer, and those who are must spend money better used to benefit the family. This is an "access to justice" issue and a pricing issue. There is a better way.

Mediation is a form of "alternate dispute resolution." It can increase "access to judgment," reduce acrimony, allow the parties to control the outcome, and set the stage for a successful "post litigation relationship."

The current rules place artificial limits and restrictions upon innovation and access of justice.

The separation of "children's issue" from property, debt, fitness, and alimony issues places a huge barrier to global resolution of contested family court cases.

Current weaknesses are: 1. Many WV Family Court Judges do not appreciate or understand the benefits of mediation; 2. In those jurisdictions, parties and lawyers are less likely to negotiate successfully; 3. Face to face meetings often deteriorate into failure; 4. Not all lawyers make the effort; and,

5. If parties were good at working out their differences, probably would not be adversaries.

So, here are some suggestions:

A.   Educate people on the benefits of mediation.

B.   Require family law lawyers to get training in negotiation and mediation. Some may become mediators, but all family lawyers need to know how to be a constructive force in mediation.

C.   Require litigants in the vast majority of family cases to participate in good faith mediation.

D.   Establish a fund for low income litigants to have mediation, and place a realistic sliding scale, one that allows competent attorneys, with staff and overhead, not practicing out of their cars, to be mediators, for litigants who are above the poverty line.

E.   Set a standard that requires lawyers to accompany their clients at this most critical stage of representation.

F.   A "contested issue" is a contested issue and should not be differentiated between children's and other issues.

G.   Mediators should be expected to draft agreements or memorandums of understanding, signed by both parties, and should file these agreements in the court file with copies to the Court.

H.   Barring fraud or coercion, or "good cause," litigants should be held to these agreements as to other contracts.

I.   Mediation should go hand in hand with "unbundled services" so that other lawyers can work with parties to prepare them for mediation or hearings without becoming "record counsel." Key to this are clear, understandable, attorney/client contracts which establish the limits of these unbundled services in plain language.

J.   Guidelines should be established for mediators who mediate for unrepresented parties, not to restrict them, but to help assure there won't be a power imbalance, coerced agreements, or agreements favoring the more assertive or articulate party.

K.   Other ideas such as family court arbitration and collaborative divorce should be researched and considered.

L.   I question and can't yet recommend "limited law licenses," but I strongly believe the range of services paralegals can supply under the supervision of a lawyer needs to be expanded.

M.   Family Court Judges should observe mediations in jurisdictions outside of their own. Until a person has participated in mediation, he or she just cannot understand the dynamic and the potential of such a non-confrontational tool.

N.   In jurisdictions where mediation is the norm, cases move quicker and dockets stay clearer. And, even though mediators and lawyers don't work for free, there are drastic cost savings when cases do not have to go to a contested trial, and appeals are reduced.

MEDIATION INTAKE FORM

What is your name? _____.

Case   Number?   _____.   Date?

_____

Do you have an attorney? _____? If so, name?

_____

_____

Please confirm you have read and understand the attached
mediation information sheet:_____

Please provide a concise list of any unresolved issues between
your and the other party: (Examples are, Primary child care,
decision making, division of your personal property, of your
real estate, or retirement benefits, and of your debts, alimony
(spousal support), or other:

_____

_____

_____

_____

_____

_____

Assuming you will be permitted to meet in separate rooms by
your mediator, and even if you have doubts that you and the
other party can resolve your differences by agreement, is there
any serious reason such as potential violence or serious health

issues that you believe should excuse you from participating in mediation? (Circle One)   No. Yes.

Other(specify): _____

_____

Thank you for your information; please add any comments or questions:

_____

_____

_____

REVISED RULES OF FAMILY COURT MEDIATION

"Burt's Proposal"

These rules supersede former Family Court Rules 38 through 46.

Whereas, family courts are becoming clogged, and our juvenile abuse and neglect system is becoming overburdened.

Whereas family court litigants are suffering problems with access to justice and speedy trial.

Whereas, the former mediation rules were restrictive, unduly pessimistic, and costly to administrate.

Whereas, "the adversary system" often does not work efficiently for families and parents and their children.

Whereas, the benefit of innovation, speed, cost savings, and dispute resolution outweigh the lawyerly compulsion to establish "rules" and "procedures."

So, therefore:

A.   Litigants and their lawyers are strongly encouraged to learn about mediation and participate.

B.   Mandatory Parenting Training will add a mediation module.

C.   Just as lawyers have many requirements, including the recent requirement for competency in the use of technology, they also will be expected to obtain training in the mediation process, at least as advocates and to educate their clients.

D.   Lawyers will be expected to be present with their clients at mediation, which is a critical stage in their representation of their clients.

E.   Keeping in mind safety (serious history of domestic violence, drug or alcohol abuse, or sexual abuse), the needs of the parties (young children, large assets or debts, disparity of income of the parties), family courts will have broad discretion in selecting mediators, making referrals, and setting the time limitations, place, and other factors.

F.   Family courts may only refer to mediators on the Court Approved list, but must keep a list of all qualified mediators and permit litigants to select their own mediator and to make private payment for those not on the Court Approved list.

G.   Barring a motion for good cause, or a stipulation, which should be viewed skeptically by the court, by counsel that mediation will be unhelpful, the family court will be expected to refer litigants to mediation. In rare instances, alternatives such as conflict counseling, or a family or pastor volunteer, may be used as an "alternate dispute resolution mechanism".

H.   Parenting plans will be expected to have an alternate dispute resolution mechanism, usually mediation.

I.   There will be no pre-mediation screening, except litigants will be required to fill out a "mediation intake form" for the courts to review prior to the hearing.

J.   The Supreme Court of Appeals expects mediation to occur in most, at least 90% of cases, and to be successful more than half the time. (Good mediators already achieve 80% and better.)

K.   Mediators will follow all previously established confidentiality standards, but they will send a copy of any signed mediated agreement, property settlement agreement, or parenting plan to the court within 48 hours after the mediation, and a report whether mediation was successful, whether each party appeared, and on time, and whether either party or both were obstructive or refused to negotiate in good faith. This requirement will NEVER be used to put undue pressure on a party who simply does not want to agree, or give up a legal right.

L.   Mediators will take every reasonable step to assure that agreements are entered into free of threats, coercion, or undue pressure and will ALWAYS caucus with the

146

parties long enough to make reasonable inquiry, and will be expected to make sure the parties have no side deals or "understandings" that are not reduced to writing.

M.   Related to these rules are concepts such as "unbundling" of legal service, limited contracts, collaborative divorce and family dispute resolution, and arbitration. These rules do not address such concepts but anticipate that innovative lawyers, judges, and mediators will explore these concepts within existing rules.

N.   When the large majority of lawyers and judges and participants find a "rule" unhelpful, that rule should be reevaluated.

5.   Self - Represented Mediation

Let me make a few things clear:

People should not be their own lawyers in family court or in pursuing their personal injury claim with an insurance company;

The average person, even with due diligence, cannot cope with the power imbalance, the myriad rules, the statutes, the case law, and the techniques necessary to prepare and negotiate their own cases;

Even with the help of a skilled mediator, there are risks for the self-represented party, whether the other party has a lawyer or not;

Even a well-prepared party will often lack the negotiating skills or emotional perspective to obtain a just agreement, and;

A failed mediation leaves the unrepresented party with all the challenges of a contested trial.

Here we will leave the subject of personal injury claims, since most of those do not go to mediation until after suit is filed, except to say, here is the link to a search of my blog for the term "personal injury." It has 109 "hits;" so I hope you enjoy it:

http://hunterlawfirm.net/?s=%22personal+injury%22

If you are still here, perhaps you are facing your own family law matter. Perhaps you are thinking of filing, have filed, or have been sued. If so, first re-read 1-5 above!

I have written an article expressly for the person who cannot or will not be hiring a lawyer: http://hunterlawfirm.net/when-you-cant-or-wont-hire-a-lawyer-a-possible-option/ . I have also written a proposal for revision of the family court and civil mediation rules: http://hunterlawfirm.net/time-revise-mediation-wv/

Recently, I came upon another approach to the problem. I was contacted by one of two self-represented parties. Not sure whether they were court ordered or had just heard of me, and, for purposes of this article, I prefer not to know. They needed a mediator for their divorce.

Each paid her and his deposit and showed up. In this instance, they agreed on what they owned, what they owed, and what they earned. They had no big dispute over valuation.

The marriage had grown stale, and they were just occupying the same space. They were not bitter, just sad.

We worked out an agreement. She thought she needed financial help for five years, but he was sure she needed it for seven. So, we set it up for seven.

Then we did a rough draft of her petition. She signed it. He filed his own answer, from the circuit clerk's office, admitting irreconcilable differences and joining in a motion to approve their agreement.

I assisted her in preparing a simple order approving it. They both signed it.

She just reported the judge was happy with the agreement and the order and approved them. They now have their "no fault" divorce. The cost? Under $1000.

Now they just want to divide his retirement for the 26 years they were together. I think I can do that, unless they are fighting over a "survivorship" provision.

Total cost for the two of them? Around $1500.

Is this pushing the envelope too far? I hope not. It used to be that a lawyer could be disbarred for "appearing to represent both parties."

I once got a final divorce decree set aside because my colleague, a former WV State Bar President, prepared the answer for the wife. A huge difference was that he really was representing the husband, who paid him, and the wife really did get screwed out of a fair settlement. And the "friendly" appearance meant she believed everything her husband told her the lawyer said, even the stuff he didn't!

But, a mediator does not represent either party. He/she is devoted to the process, to guiding them towards a fair compromise. The limits of what a mediator can do for them are not fully defined. They need to be explored and, I believe, pushed beyond what we are doing now.

I said in a recent blog article that I am chair of The WV State Bar Board of Governors' committee on the future of the law, and I recently attended a very "hi-tech," cutting edge, seminar organized by www.The Lawyerist.com on the future of the law called "TDBLaw" in St. Louis Mo.,

http://hunterlawfirm.net/future-of-the-law-2016/ .

I also have read the ABA report and the N.C. Law Review Vol. 67 on the major areas of "the future of the law."

The views expressed here are my personal views and not the those of any bar association or group.

One idea that is gaining ground is "unbundling" of legal services. Here is an example.

What is wrong for a party or parties, if he/she/they are not going to hire a lawyer, to go to a trained mediator? If;

They are essentially in agreement? Or,

There are clear, even strong, differences, but there is civility?

I say, "Nothing.," but I have a counter to the implications of that question.

Often, one or both may not be candid about emotional or physical abuse, drug or alcohol abuse, or have a "secret" that one holds over the other.

How can the mediator guarantee that she/he will not end up facilitating an unfair agreement?

Answer? She can't!

But, in a state with 70% of the litigants unrepresented in family court, with drug abuse rampant, with overworked judges who are lucky to spend 30-60 minutes with the parties before deciding their fate and their children's, isn't it better to have them spend a few hours with a trained facilitator?

I say, "Yes!" to that too. I propose that WV mediators and judges push the limits of mediation for un-represented parties.

I also propose that lawyers be permitted to provide as little as an hour of her/his time in meeting with a party in helping them prepare for mediation.

Here are a few caveats:

A.   A mediator must be prepared to back off or not prepare documents when he/she "smells a rat."

B.   A mediator must be prepared to announce that the parties really should have lawyers and to explain why.

C.   A mediator must get signed waivers if the mediator is going to "ghost write" a pleading to be signed by just one of them. And I am dubious that the mediator can draft the responsive pleading. Personally, I think that should be allowed, assuming both parties agree.

D.   A mediator who is going to experiment with this kind of unbundling must have fine "antennae" and excellent mediation skills and family law expertise. It is not a job for sissies.

In short, just as we are not supposed to take on a case we are not trained for, we should not be tackling mediation we are not qualified for.

I am comfortable with the one mediation I have done this way to date, and am posting this with the hope of getting some feedback from colleagues, even judges, or members of the WV State Bar.

I thank my friend Scott for his insightful and constructive comments, and to my wife for listening to them.

6.   So You Aren't Going to Mediation! (Now what will you do?)

This article is aimed primarily at family court lawyers, but lay people may benefit.

Let's keep something in mind. Personal injury and civil mediation are different from family mediation. People are representing themselves in family court perhaps 70% of the time and somehow surviving. There are mandatory forms, parenting classes, and a form of "one size fits all justice." I do not recommend it, but it's happening.

I have dealt with self-representation (pro se) in family court elsewhere.

http://hunterlawfirm.net/?s=%22self+representation%22+or+%22pro+se%22

Circuit Court is no place for the self-represented (pro se) litigant! Danger lurks there.

So let's focus on family court. Under what situations will family court litigants not go to mediation? Here are some examples:

A.   The Family Court does not send them, or the Court's "Case Coordinator" screens them out. It happens all too often.

B.   The parties can't afford mediation but don't qualify for free mediation.

C.   The parties are litigating in a part of the State where lawyers do not typically mediate their cases.

D.   Or the litigation is in a part of the state where parties' lawyers tend not to attend mediation!

I am a strong proponent of mediation in family court and civil court and am sorry it is not used in other kinds of cases. But what if it just is not going to happen? Let's consider negotiated settlement, especially face to face settlement meetings.

A.   Court mandated face to face settlement meetings can be powder kegs. Family Court "screens for mediation" but not for these much more volatile and dangerous meetings! Judges should be made to watch some of those fiascos!

B.   We family law lawyers who mediate a lot tend to lose our appetite for "face to face." Guess we are "spoiled."

C.	Even in mediation, we tend to caucus before the initial greeting and send the mediator back and forth. But, if there is no mediator, what to do?

D.	I suggest to my colleagues that in those cases we need to sharpen our negotiating skills.

E.	I find written offers back and forth wasteful and unproductive.

F.	But, the era of meeting with the client, dictating the offer, typing it up, affixing a stamp, waiting for the pony to deliver it, making an appointment with the client, reviewing the offer, dictating a response, typing it up, affixing a stamp, and sending the pony back, is over. Those were dark ages for written negotiations.

G.	Now we can type the offer with the client present, copy the client, and perhaps send offers and counter offers 2, 3 times in a day. For the right parties and the right lawyers that can work, but the old model was broken and is outmoded. It took weeks to do what we can do in mediation in an hour.

H.	If we are going to meet and negotiate, we must get new tools and sharpen the old ones.

I.	Read, read, read, how to negotiate. And attend continuing legal education. It is a skill we can learn. It is a skill we can polish. If you do not train to learn to negotiate, you will be terrible at it.

J.	Somehow figure out how to make your case w/o alienating the other side.

K.   Do not overreact, especially if the other side is ham-handed. Many lawyers became lawyers because they were born ham-handed! From my experience with younger lawyers, I fear they are teaching truculence in law school.

L.   If you are easily intimidated, this line of work may not be for you. There is no bailiff, and bullies exist. I am not a bully, but bullies don't affect me. That's a strength, I hope. There are good women negotiators. They can deflect and shame the bully. The best of us use what God gave us.

M.   Be prepared! Here are some ideas:

     i.   The court rules require full financial disclosure and a list of witnesses and exhibits. Share and bring your documentation!

     ii.   Printed balances of all monetary accounts, at time of separation and now.

     iii.   Printed balances of all unpaid financial obligations, then and now. Documentation of bills you have paid.

     iv.   Have printed values of all retirement plans, pensions, IRA's, 401 K's, profit sharing.

     v.   If it is "defined benefit" plan, meaning it does not have a balance but has a "present value" based on actuarial principles, see if you can get that present value from the "plan administrator" or a forensic accountant. Family businesses often are worth little beyond the income the owner takes.

vi. If there is a family business, you have work to do figuring out its value or be prepared to sell the assets and divide the proceeds. You may need to hire a business valuation expert. In that event, you had better have a lawyer and had better budget for mediation! I like to propose to share the cost of appraisers and use one for each kind of property instead of two. Real estate, personal property, and businesses are three kinds of appraisers. Perhaps an auctioneer.

vii. If alimony is an issue, identify the factors, from the 20 enumerated by the statute, that impact the length, amount, and nature of the alimony. Fault is only one factor.

viii. Find a formula, Judge Goldberg's, the Va. formula, or something that you can hang your calculation on. If your judge uses one, you better find out which one and prepare.

ix. Come to the table with constructive "win-win" ideas. That is essential.

x. Be wary about separating the parties and walking back and forth. Your client can imagine all manner of nefarious sell-outs going on in that other room. She/he is thinking, "You are letting that bastard/bitch 'snow you' ." I have learned not to do it.

xi.   Have the tools to create the documents, the Property Settlement Agreement, Parenting Plan, and Final Order. I use document assembly software that is compatible with Microsoft Word, Pathagoras, to "fill in the blanks" and print near final drafts. You should too!

xii.   For custody issues, you must know how to calculate child support, carefully prepare necessary caretaking functions worksheets for the one and two years prior to separation, have the children's medical records if relevant, and have a detailed list of concerns and goals. It is imperative to have a good parenting plan template.

xiii. Again, if there are abuse issues, substance or domestic, serious alimony issues, or substantial property or debt, why are you there without a lawyer? You are over your head!

xiv.   If lawyers did these things, many cases would not require a mediator, but a good mediator can smooth the bumps, keep abrasive lawyers apart, filter the insults, and even insist on taking breaks to obtain more facts, online or by phone.

xv.   Mediators can make up for the faults of the litigants and their lawyers and they can become an ally of the lawyer in helping the party assess risk benefit. Good lawyers and mediators NEVER put undue pressure on a party.

xvi. IN SUMMARY, well prepared litigants with positive attitudes, and competent lawyers with negotiating skills are perfect compliments to competent mediators. Together they can be a power team in achieving a negotiated settlement. So, mediate, mediate, mediate, but if no mediation, learn how to negotiate! Where possible, hire a good lawyer!

VI.
FUTURE OF THE LAW, ACCESS TO JUSTICE, AND LAW OFFICE MANAGEMENT

1. A Few Thoughts on Law Office Technology

Technology is a "two-edged sword." It can be a time waster. It is easy for someone like me to "gamify" technology, so the very acts of using it and learning from it provide surges of dopamine pleasure which divert me from the actual boring tasks at hand.

And, social media has a "siren's song." It is serious work to keep social media from being a time waster. When well done, it is a life enhancer.

But, it also causes me to look back on a wonderful two-day seminar like the 59th annual West Virginia Association for Justice Annual Meeting and Seminar knowing that I missed 25 % or 30 % of what I should have learned because I was tending to things back in the office, looking up things that the author was talking about, and even writing emails to the presenter. And it is a great time to update and reorganize the apps on my iPad desktop!

It can also allow me to write three rough drafts of blog articles using Nuance's' "Dragon Anywhere" in fifteen minutes while waiting for my wife to finish up at church.

I went through approximately 15 versions of Dragon Naturally Speaking, each one promising "this is the one that really works," until I got to a point where it truly enhances my ability to get things done. The new versions are "Dragon Professional" and "Dragon Anywhere," $150 each.

I estimate the accuracy to be approximately five times that of Siri's voice to text and twice as good as "Dragon Go."

Yesterday I met with a returning client. Her reconciliation efforts had failed. We already have her divorce petition and motion for temporary relief, but, using the built-in questionnaire and features of the document assembly application "Pathagoras," I was able to rough out her parenting plan agreement, property settlement agreement, and final divorce order in our initial two hour meeting. The key is using consistent "variable labels," so that a saved database of information entered into the first form can fill in the same "variables" in the others.

It is a generalization, but the family law bar is not a coherent group. The family law lawyers don't meet regularly, they don't market themselves well, and they don't take well to technology. There are exceptions, especially in the larger urban areas where the divorce lawyers who cater to the doctors and bankers and the lawyers can make pretty good money and use it for staff and technology. While no family law colleague has refused my request to borrow a form, I have failed to get the family bar to develop Pathagoras form banks. Our clients are the losers!

I take satisfaction in knowing that my use of technology, our office systems, and our trained staff allow me to keep fees much lower than other similar experienced counsel.

In the last three months, as I phased-out of some out-of-office activities such as seminar presentations, board membership, and other activities, we have made some real breakthroughs in our technology which I intend to carry through for the next 10 years, hoping to complete 55 years in the practice of law and to finish on a high note. Technology will be a key.

2.   A Concise Summary of the Future of the Law

I tackled this subject last summer in a major article, perhaps 1500 words. It is an important subject, but I took on too much.

I tried to:

Establish my credentials;

Summarize my trip to the TBD Conference in Saint Louis;

To report to my WV State Bar Board of Governors' "Future of the Law" Committee, and:

To discuss tips and techniques to improve law office efficiency.

Here is where to find that article should you have the stomach for it: [2]http://hunterlawfirm.net/future-of-the-law-2016/.

So, let's get to the point. Recently I listened to a panel on the Joshua Johnson (replacement of Diane Rehm) radio show. It credibly reported that Uber drivers are no more secure than video store owners were. With the owner/drivers being nearly 70 % of Uber's business expense, and renting themselves and their cars, soon Uber and its industry will own a huge fleet of self-driving cars. Even if they are twice the cost of current cars, Uber can save 1/3!

One of the speakers suggested that lawyers are on the same track as Uber drivers, and, I might add, coal miners, buggy whip manufacturers, and checkout clerks.

I also heard Judge Neil Gorsuch, in his testimony before Congress, on the failings of the legal industry to provide access to justice for millions. He criticized our profession for resisting change and innovations such as Legal Zoom and AVVO and suing to keep them out of our states. I might add, resistance to using paralegals much as the medical profession uses PA's and Nurse Practitioners.

He explained that our profession "is not well" and that it has a high level of suicide and alcohol and drug abuse. I have been talking about that a lot in my blog, which I hope is oriented towards the future. I have not had much impact.

Courageous leadership in the ABA has been leading a study on the means of expanding and reducing the costs of legal services. They are supporting "disruption innovation," new ways of thinking and approaching problems. I concur.

I have been trying to repackage some services, unbundling and ghostwriting for people who just cannot find $3000- $10,000 to hire a family law lawyer. [3]http://hunterlawfirm.net/when-you-cant-or-wont-hire-a-lawyer-a- possible- option/

I have written a proposal to streamline mediation in WV, [4]http://hunterlawfirm.net/time-revise-mediation- wv/, and how self-represented people could use well qualified mediators to protect their children and interests, http://hunterlawfirm.net/self-represented-mediation/

Some things appear not to be on our radar. Our WV legislature, as I write this, is well on the way to decimating consumer protection law in WV and taking away incentive of lawyers to be able to represent these aggrieved people.

Forced arbitration, which could be a solution, is a sham, designed by big business to keep consumers from suing them, and they are succeeding.

With contingent fee cases, personal injury, industrial injury, medical malpractice, and insurance bad faith, the lawyers are motivated because there are prospects of good pay days if the lawyer will delay receiving payment and accept a percentage of the final settlement or judgment.

Of course, conservatives are working to limit the percentage the contingent fee lawyer can charge. Getting to the point ain't easy, so I will close with this summary.

We aren't in a "period of change;" we are in a "period of ACCELERATING CHANGE"!

Lawyers, like all children in school right now, need to plan on lifelong learning. Much of it will be online. Sadly, it is likely there will be fewer ivy covered campuses.

3. Low Tech Fundamentals of Operating a Law Firm

http://hunterlawfirm.net/low-tech-fundamentals-of-running-a-law-office/

I recently completed an article setting out my efforts to

create an Internet presence.

http://hunterlawfirm.net/social-media-annual-review-marketing-for-the-small-firm-lawyer/

It occurred to me that my technology works because I have the underlying "bones" or foundation for a well-run office.

This article should be helpful for a new, or a struggling, lawyer. It should be helpful to an established lawyer if that lawyer has been "going through the motions," or mindlessly doing things "the old way," or who just wants to share ideas.

It is critical, in the daily hustle, to step back and consider our goals and how we can achieve those goals.

Here are some suggestions, in no particular order. Call (304 472-7477) or write hunterjb@hunterlawfirm.net if you have any questions.

Communication is a key, so here are a few tips:

A.   When you have to write someone and be able to convince the Court you reached them or at least tried in good faith, send it regular mail, and certified mail – return receipt, and attach a "certificate of service." A "certificate of service" is a written statement, signed by the lawyer, of the type of mail he used, the recipient, the address, and the date. Even if the recipient refuses to sign for the certified mail (as they do approximately half the time), the fact the regular mail does NOT come back, and that you tried both methods, will almost always satisfy the court, at least as to your good faith. And, since people are often reluctant to sign the return receipt card, it greatly increases the likelihood your message will be read.

B. Use e-mail thoughtfully. Lawyers may not communicate directly with a represented party. That is unethical. So, while not listing the opposing party in the address line, I find that e-mail is still a very effective method to communicate, with no additional cost for copying your own client, your paralegal, and blind copying your other staff, receptionist, billing, timekeeping, so they know what is happening in the case. You can include your expert, your co-counsel, the guardian ad litem (lawyer appointed to represent an infant or person under a "legal disability"), the clerk of the court, and, in juvenile abuse and neglect cases, "child protective services." It is especially helpful that your "expert" be kept informed of developments, and that your client's own insurance representatives know the status of a claim. By keeping everyone in the loop, you can move a case forward, "tickle" those who don't have their own "tickler" system, and foster better communication. I "copy to" others even when we use "snail mail," believing the small extra cost is worth it.

C. Follow up your communications: I mentioned a "tickler system" above. Space prevents a discussion of powerful practice management applications. Mine is "self-made" and harks back to my "Appleworks" suite of spreadsheet, database, task, contacts and calendar which I devised in 1981!

D. Here is the rule: NOTHING GOES OUT WITHOUT HAVING A REVIEW DATE, 2, 3, or 4 weeks out.

E. AND, one or two people in the office is/are tasked with reviewing the daily "suspense file" at the beginning of EVERY work day. This simple rule, ignored by many of my colleagues, is a key to staying on top of things.

F.   Want a " '70's" way to do this? Just get a plastic bankers box. Put 31 hanging folders into it. Number the folders 1-31. Put your file copy of the days mailings into the appropriate slot, 2,3, or 4 weeks away. Then, 14, 21, or 28 days later, your staff will pull the document(s) in the folder(s) and act on it

G.   Most will be filed (if an appropriate reply or action has happened) or an automatic follow-up date created.

H.   Staff should be trained that if 2-3 follow ups have been "suspensed" and no reply received, to alert the attorney.

I.   I usually persist by referencing and attaching the multiple requests we have made.

J.   The recipient and I know that these long strings of requests may eventually reach a judge or reviewing authority. So, better to document, document, and document your efforts to get a reply.

K.   I try never to make a threat that I am not prepared to carry out, and, as for threats, remember that just getting a letter from a lawyer can be a threat. There is no need to be accusatory or heavy handed.

L.   When I told my former USAF JAG office secretary, Cathy, in 1992, that I still followed the system that she taught me in 1972, she laughed and said, "Oh, we have used a computerized calendaring program for years!

166

Now we do too, but whatever "suspense system" you use, must be reliable.

M.   Another great tip: CHECKLISTS!

As you will learn if you read "The Checklist Manifesto" by Atul Gawande, every system benefits by meticulously thought out checklists. We have checklists for :

i.   Hearings;

ii.   Phone conferences;

iii.   Meetings with clients:

iv.   Mediation;

v.   File opening;

vi.   File maintenance;

vii.   File closing;

viii. Personal injury claims management;

ix.   Appeals, and;

x.   Many more.

N.   Forms: We have dozens of forms:

i.   Intake forms;

ii.   Telephone intake;

iii.   Organizing the facts in a case. They are the three "legs" of a solid stool:

iv.   Object list worksheets;

v.   "Burt's top ten lists" of concerns, goals, and questions.

vi.   The timeline.

vii.   Family Court Forms:

viii.   Financial affidavits;

ix.   Blank parenting plans;

x.   Application for service of the Bureau of Child Support Enforcement (B.C.S.E.);

xi.   Caretaking Functions worksheets;

xii.   Equitable Distribution worksheets;

xiii.   Proposed Equitable Distribution Spreadsheets (prepared by the lawyer using Microsoft Excel, with the client, and submitted to the court and the other party before mediation.)

O.   And we have dozens of handouts for clients (It helps to have 250 blog articles "in the can.") My stuff isn't "copywrited." Any colleague can "borrow" them.

i.   Mr. Hunter's letter to new clients, explaining who he is and how he and his staff interact with clients.

ii.   Legal Checklist: a listing of items that most people must attend to, powers of attorney, medical powers of attorney, wills, insurance limits review, potential legal controversies. My years as a Preventive Law Officer in the USAF JAG Corp. helped my approach to preventing legal problems.

iii.   "How to Organize the Facts in Your Case;"

iv.   How to avoid problems in your family law, personal injury, and civil dispute case relative to "social media;"

v.   "The Law of Equitable Distribution in WV;"

vi.   The factors considered by the court in determining alimony;

vii.   What NOT to do during the process of your divorce;

viii. What to do and not to do in the process of your personal injury claim or civil suit.

ix.   Specific warnings regarding Social Media; and,

x.   Many, many others.

P. My personal tips:

i.   Dress appropriately. There are days for blue jeans, but hearings and mediation require coat and tie.

ii.   I come to work by 7:00 a.m. on most mornings, and have a two-hour head start on most of my competitors.

iii.   I have several capable staff members to delegate work to.

iv.   I try NOT to bawl someone out for mistakes while taking on new challenges. My better employees are not afraid of me, or of taking risks, nor should they be.

v.   I keep my staff supplied with the best technology we can afford.

vi.   I reward them for getting our clients to write favorable reviews. It is not natural for them to ask for a review.

vii.   I show great flexibility for my staffs' personal schedules and obligations. They appreciate that and are committed to covering for each other.

viii.   I have a "secretaries' fund," a percentage of our gross receipts, that goes into a fund, distributed at the end of the year. It is a decent retirement plan and something most small firms do not have.

ix.   We have always provided our staff medical insurance.

x.   We treat each other like family. I am not a patient man, but I am told I am a good teacher, and some even imply I am a good boss.

Q.   Finally, the members of this firm are driven to serve
       and make lives better. We also want to make money,
       so our goals are:

       i.   Serve the clients and their families;

       ii.   Maintain a sterling reputation;

       iii.   Trust that the clients and the money will flow
               from numbers 1 and 2.

Have methods, checklists, systems, facilities, equipment, and
procedures to let us accomplish these goals.

4.   Why Should My Lawyer Know Technology?

A.   I have written on the need for lawyers (and clients) to
       use technology, I hesitated to write this, but perhaps a
       summary will help you choose a competent lawyer:

B.   A lawyer who brags of his or her ignorance of
       technology, I have found, is often rationalizing and
       justifying not putting forth the effort;

C.   Can one imagine a lawyer, or his staff, not using a word
       processor or fax machine? Of course not.

D.   Faxes are almost gone. Think scanned images, digital
       faxes, and e-mail.

E.   80% of my serious correspondence is now numbered,
       concise paragraphs in an e-mail.

F.   Think about it:

     i.   -The client calls or write with a question;

     ii.   -The paralegal forwards to the lawyer;

     iii.   -The lawyer writes his response/suggestion;

     iv.   -He copies the client, the opposing lawyer, his paralegal, the scheduling clerk, and his billing clerk.

     v.   -Or he may ask the paralegal to scan and send a document, or call the client, or draft a letter, or even make coffee.

     vi.   -A few minutes later, the client or opposing lawyer responds. That message is forwarded to interested persons.

     vii.   -Within the hour the challenge is solved. We do that several dozen times a week! Perhaps the client's week-end with his daughter is saved, a change has been negotiated, a subrogation claim taken care of, or a real estate transaction concluded.

G.   The lawyer with Dropbox, iCloud , Google's Cloud Service, Evernote, etc., can carry your file to trial on his laptop.

H.   The lawyer with World Docs or Carbonite can have his entire office on his laptop, iPad, or other device.

I.   The lawyer with a new iPad or iPhone, has Siri to create reminders and calendar entries, or to find restaurants or hotels.

J.   Fourteen WV Counties are testing a pilot program of "e-filing" of lawsuits and their pleadings; some county courthouse records are online and others will follow.

K.   Lawyers with the CaseSoft software suite can scan or upload transcripts, index the transcripts, send testimony to "CaseMap, link testimony to key issues, and use the stored material to draft pre-trial memos and orders.

L.   Lawyers who use Excel can create equitable distribution spreadsheets of his client's debts and assets, prepare a proposed distribution, and show the client how close his proposal, or the other side's, is to a fifty percent/fifty percent distribution split.

M.   Lawyers who use Dragon can dictate less formal documents on the fly with "voice to print."

N.   Lawyers with Pathagoras document assembly can fill in questionnaires and e-mail clients' pleadings or documents to his paralegal for final editing.

O.   Lawyers with online legal research have an edge in timing and accuracy.

P.   Lawyers who use outliners can create efficient litigation outlines and task lists.

Q.   Lawyers who blog can create innumerable "handouts," forms, and instruction sheets for their clients.

R.	Lawyers with a compact digital camera/camcorder, can back up the accident reconstructionist, photograph injuries, "scan" documents and photos into their smart phones, get Google images of collision scenes, and take screen shots of texts, e-mail, photographs, and graphics. But, don't forget to "take a class" if you are not already a pretty decent and experienced amateur photographer.

S.	Lawyers with sophisticated "practice management systems" and "billing and bookkeeping applications" can print reports, analyze cash flow and profitability, streamline billing, increase revenues, and improve efficiency.

T.	But, even a simple spreadsheet can show what percentage of income and expenses go for staff, equipment, insurance, utilities, and other necessaries.

U.	Another spreadsheet can show how many dollars per hour the lawyer makes in various practice areas.

V.	A smartphone with "hosted Outlook" or something similar carries the office calendar, alarms, task lists, contact list, e-mails, and text messaging.

W.	My iPhone is a dictating machine, a camera, a camcorder, a scanner, a GPS, and much, much more. (Almost forgot – it is also a phone!)

X.	A lawyer who shares, shares, shares, communicates, connects, and facilitates with clients, potential clients, friends, and family:

	i.	Has a fascinating and stimulating life;

ii.   Keeps friends and relationships that others lose.

iii.   Uses his blogs to create good will, build his practice, improve the profession, feed his ego, show off a bit, and keep everything from his kindergarten, high school, and college class groups, his military buddies, family, and community or church choir, together.

Y.   A lawyer with a couple of e-readers, say a Kindle and an iPad, has the knowledge of the world at his fingertips, and he can stream music, radio, and movies.

Z.   A lawyer who loves to read and reads broadly, has sources of wisdom for every occasion. And he can bore and offend his friends with his reading list.

AA.   In Summary, a lawyer who embraces technology and the future will have one less subject to gripe about as he becomes a lovable curmudgeon.

5.   Low Tech Time Management

A.   The book *Effective Time Management* (Using Outlook); Seiwert and Woeltje

B.   Eisenhower Matrix: p.p. 38-43.

C.   I have seen this in other forms, but the basics are simple, but hard to stick to.

D.   Urgent And Important : DO IT OR SCHEDULE TIME TO DO IT!

E.   Urgent But Not Important: the daily tasks we "have to" do, but are usually more important to the person putting the demand on you. (Deal with it, delegate, quick e-mail reply, or schedule a part of your day, but realize what they are. Sometimes just say no.

F.   IMPORTANT but not urgent.

     i.   These are the new office system you are working on, the form file you were going to create, or the book you are going to write.

     ii.   Fight, fight, fight, to set aside time for your IMPORTANT but not urgent tasks, and give your staff time to do them, and explain this system to them. (I use e-mail to deal with these, copying others, but e-mail does create or allow more of them.

     iii.   HAVE important but not urgent projects. That's how you progress in life and in your profession.

     iv.   The same principle works at home, building that deck, planting that flower bed, etc.

6.   When You Cannot or Will Not Hire A Lawyer:

A $500 OPTION

A.   **First; let's define the kind of case.** If it is a fault-based personal injury claim, such as serious injuries resulting from a rear end collision, the kindest think I can say to a person who tries to document and settle that case without counsel is "foolish." Forget your pre-conceptions and just give me a call. You will learn a lot, at no financial risk.

B. **In those cases, the lawyer works for no fee until the money is collected.** Most charge 25%-33 1/3% of any sum(s) recovered, but our firm takes just 20% if fault is not seriously contested. You simply don't know how to document, argue, or settle your claim. DON'T do it.

C. **And, if you have a case involving $10,000 or more,** being tried in circuit court, **you CAN'T do it because you:**

    i.   **Don't know the Trial Court Rules:**

    ii.   **Don't know the Rules of Evidence;**

    iii.   **Don't know The Rules of Civil Procedure,**

    iv.   **Don't know the Rules of Appellate Procedure;**

    v.   **Don't know the Statutory Law, and,**

    vi.   **Don't know the Case Law.**

D. I have devised a $500 option for family and civil suit parties.

    i.   **The personal injury claimant is the easiest.** I will talk to them for an hour or so **for free.** If it is a case I am willing to take, the claimant virtually always hires me. Quite simply, I know what I am doing, have lots of experience, have answers to their questions, and have a good facility and great staff. **Problem solved.**

ii.　　**But, people who can't afford, or refuse to hire, a lawyer now have one more option.**

E.　　I have developed a method to provide maximum assistance, as a consultant not record counsel, for the flat sum of $500.

F.　　What? "I've heard divorces cost between $3000-$10,000?!"

G.　　You are right. Some lawyers have built reputations partly by charging a large retainer, $5000 or more. This puzzles me, but people figure, "You get what you pay for." Do they really think such lawyers will move aggressively for an early negotiated settlement? That has not been my experience.

H.　　A typical retainer for a person who was married for ten years, has a 401K, house with mortgage, cars, job, and children is $2850. I will usually keep at least $1050, but will do $3050 work of work and service before charging more, and, if we go over that sum, I reduce my hourly rate from $250 to $200. That way we "share the pain" of a contested divorce.

I.　　Most divorces are not contested; because:

i.　　**I negotiate aggressively**, using mediation often; and because,

ii.   **My opponent in trial is dealing with someone who has tried hundreds of cases,** and that's not cheap or fun! Most people want to avoid that.

J.   **However,** if you have a family business, multiple assets, substance abuse, violence, or alimony issues, lawyers' **fees and costs can grow exponentially.**

K.   **For $500, I will give you access to all the rules** referenced above, provide our proprietary forms, and provide the forms required by the Court.

L.   **We will copy for you applicable statutes and WV case-law.** You must know the rules of the game if you expect to play.

M.   **You can fill out your forms in our office, and we will look them over.**

N.   **If you and your spouse have substantially worked out your differences,** for another $500 or so, total @ $1000, we can also prepare a property settlement agreement (PSA),permanent parenting plan (PPA), and Final Decree. This happens in my office 2-3 times a year, but when it happens, people can be divorced in 30 days or less!

O.   **But, please understand, a "consultant" is not going into court with you.** If the judge does not approve your agreement(s), you may be "back to square one." We try to draft agreements acceptable to the court, but we can't guarantee the Court will understand your explanation or approve your agreement(s). And, while the Family Court is used to having self-represented litigants, the circuit court definitely is not.

P. **My "consultation" includes a free PDF file of my "Blog Book" and other documents stored on a thumb drive.** It is our compilation of most of my blog articles, *"Perspectives of a Small-Town Lawyer"* and *"WV Lawyer, Tips and Techniques."* It contains over 500 pages containing things I have learned in over 40 years.

Q. **These consultations are not based on an hourly rate,** but we do not charge beyond that without an additional "fee agreement" **and** unless the total effort exceeds our normal hourly rate. **Such a "consultation" is the result of years of experience, and hundreds of hours of preparation. What we provide is limited, but considerable.**

R. **We have two articles on "How to Organize The Facts In Your Case."** and forms to use in gathering the information.

S. **Truth in advertising:** many of the people who hire me as a consultant realize they cannot risk being without a lawyer, so they decide to hire me as their record counsel.

T. **And, some people, for $500-$1050, end up with expedited, fair, comprehensive, agreements and final orders.**

U. **Even the person who moves forward, in trepidation, without a lawyer** receives "the rules of the game," an assessment of the risks, and solid, basic advice on how to move their case forward and get along with the judge. No guarantees, but better than nearly complete ignorance.

V. **So, if you know someone who can't afford to hire a lawyer,** has become discouraged by quoted retainers, or is too stubborn to hire counsel, he/she can get a full consultation for a small fraction of the cost of a contested trial.

This method is not perfect, but I believe it is consistent with CLE presentations I have attended where lawyers are encouraged to figure a way to represent indigent and low-income people and to "think outside of the box" in providing legal services.

7. Unbundling of Legal Services - A Low Cost Alternative

The poor and people of moderate income have great difficulty in obtaining legal services in WV. Something like 70% of litigants in family court are "pro-se" or self-represented.

For a while, WV was in the dark ages. There was an ethics opinion that lawyers couldn't even "ghost write," or assist a party from behind, without becoming "record counsel."

That has been clarified. We now can do those things. Unfortunately, contrary to more progressive states, WV does not allow special appearance or special pleadings. Once a lawyer's name is declared as representative, there is a very specific procedure the lawyer must do to extricate herself.

Here is a very informative Podcast from "New Solo," host Adriana Linares, on The Legal Talk network: [1]http://j.mp/2omGi5q

The idea is for experienced and competent lawyers to do what they can do, prepare forms, coach, "ghost- write," counsel, and educate the unrepresented party for 1/5th to 1/10th of the cost of full representation.

Here are two products I have constructed:

"The Legal Checkup": this works for individuals and couples who need simple wills, powers of attorney, and review of legal matters such a boundary dispute with a neighbor or quarrel over Mom's estate: http://hunterlawfirm.net/your-legal-checkup-and-review/

When you are a family court litigant, http://hunterlawfirm.net/when-you-cant-or-wont-hire-a-lawyer-a-possible-option/ .

The "Legal Checkup" client often only needs that simple will and power of attorney and review of her or their insurance coverages.

About half the time, the family court litigant who is not ready to retain a lawyer, realizes during the consultation that he/she can come up with the funds, and retains me to appear on their behalf. As Sam Glover of *The Lawyerist* Podcast says, "What do you have to lose?" https://lawyerist.com/podcast/

8.   Suggestions for Operating and Marketing A Small Firm Efficiently and on a Budget

Except for a four-year stint in a firm called the U.S. Air Force JAG Corp, I have been in firms of no more than 3 lawyers for over 40 years.

As a sole practitioner, I have had 3-5 assistants. When a valued employee decided to become a stay at home wife and mother, I was pleased that we were able to stay just as efficient with four as we had with five.

Now that my family law paralegal extraordinaire became Upshur County Assistant Administrator, it isn't easy for us to be down to three, but I am hoping our technology will allow us to do that.

My goal today is to give you some practical ideas, not all of which are law office technology, but not to overwhelm you.

A word of explanation about my blog. Eight years ago, I began to put into writing the things I had learned in almost 50 years of legal practice. I decided to share what they call "green" or rich content with potential clients, colleagues, judges, and even law school and college professors.

I decided that I could contribute, and that it was the way I wanted to shape my "brand" and professional image. I have tried to "share" more than self-promote. In the last three years, I have served on the WV State Bar Board of Governors, the WV Assoc. for Justice Board of Governors, chaired the State Bar BOG Middle and High School Video Competition, chaired and served on the State Bar BOG "Future of the Law Committee," and served on the WV State Bar Family Law Committee and Family Law Mediation Subcommittee. All have been valuable learning experiences.

I have also written on low tech office management techniques: http://hunterlawfirm.net/low-tech-fundamentals-of-running-a-law-office/

I want to stress something: I could stop now and simply go over with you the contents of this "how to" article. **If you are 30 years old, I urge you to read it.** It is how I do things, day after day, year after year. And it is NOT "rocket science." If you fail to deal with your inbox, digital and physical, EVERY day, you will fall behind. You will have to come up with excuses. You will borrow from Peter to pay Paul. And you will hear from State Bar Disciplinary Counsel. Remember, we in small firms are the ones Disciplinary Counsel zooms in on. We are perceived as vulnerable, and many of us fall short. Fight, Fight, Fight, to maintain the standards your spouse, children, grandchildren, friends, and ethical colleagues want you to.

Watch out for stress, substances that give short-term relief and long-term grief. And care, care, care about the people who trust and rely on you to protect them.

You know what you are interested in or want to improve. I will provide resources for office management, office technology, time management, case preparation, document assembly, client relations, and branding or marketing, and the use of social media. There's a lot here, so pick and choose what's right for you.

Let me remind you of some essentials that I have learned from nationally recognized seminar speakers during the last seven years:

A.   You must have a computer, with at least Windows 10 or the current Apple iOS.

B.   You need a horizontal screen <u>and</u> a portrait screen for your heavy-duty work. If two screens are good; three are better. I have five at the office, connected to two Windows 10 machines, and two iDevices.

C. You must be saving data off site. And, assuming you still <u>use</u> paper, don't <u>save</u> paper closed files. Save electronically and return paper files to the client, or shred them.

D. There are a few competitors, but I say you need a Fujitsu Scansnap sheet-feed scanner; (send to scanned documents to e-mail, Scansnap Organizer, Evernote, Dropbox, One-Note, or to a file.)

E. You need to have good mobile equipment, iPhone and iPad preferably, and the ability to dictate and send memos and orders back to the office with voice to text. I use Dictamus for audio files, Dragon Anywhere for my phone, and Nuance Dragon Professional (Individual) with headset at my office desk.

F. You must be able to save, search, and manipulate data, text, photos, videos, audio!

G. So, get online. I suggest http://lynda.com or www.Udemy.com and take a course in Windows 10. While you are at it, I have found a course in Microsoft Word to be very helpful.

H. See my "Caveats" article which I wrote shortly after completing two seminar outlines: http://hunterlawfirm.net/cle-caveat-9-24-2015/

I. You must know what "The Cloud" is, and you must have a strategy. If your office burns down tomorrow, can you open two days later in a new location? Are you saving paper client files? If so, some day you will regret it.

RESOURCES: WV Legal Sites

I insert here three important websites from the WV Legal Community, two of which I had formerly overlooked:

Young Lawyers: http://www.wvyounglawyers.com/

Legal Aid of WV: http://www.lawv.net/

WV State Bar and related Links: http://www.wvbar.org/

My blog, now a combination of what used to be two blogs, "Perspectives of a Small-Town Lawyer," and "WV Lawyer - Tips and Techniques," is searchable, just type your term(s) into the search window. -

For example, you will get 98 "hits" (Editor's note: now 98 hits) by entering the search term "mediation," and yes, I voice strong opinions and the bases for my opinions on civil and family mediation. http://hunterlawfirm.net/?s=Mediation

My e-book is a downloadable PDF file. It has a table of contents, 350 articles, and 1100 pages It has posts on office management, law office technology, personal injury, mediation, insurance law, family law, civil litigation, my ideas of new products we can sell, and my larger views of the world. http://hunterlawfirm.net/book.pdf

YOUR SOCIAL MEDIA AND INTERNET PRESENCE

I am going to tell you exactly what my sources say you need to create a formidable web presence with a combination of a website, paid services, print media, and social media.

We recently added a button to my website linked to "Our Reviews" and are working hard to demote "Jaynajane's" assessment of me: "Incompetent at Best - This guy is an overpriced arrogant jerk." I will be discussing how to establish your brand and promote and protect your reputation online

My articles reflect my personality and my interests.

I try to provide value laced with humor.

For example:

"Buy a Million Dollar Umbrella": provides insights into avoiding financial ruin and filling a critical gap in your insurances. This one I got from my friend and expert Vince King, whose memorandum and research helped me find $ 1.2 million in UIM coverage. http://hunterlawfirm.net/buy-a-1000000-umbrella/

Regarding gaps in coverages. Do not learn too late that your liability claim from your devastating car wreck is not covered under your underinsured, UIM, coverage! It is stunning to think there are lawyers in WV driving around with personal umbrellas that do not provide UIM coverage. Check with your carrier!

9.   Pathagoras Segment - Roy Lasris

Today I will share 15 minutes of my time with Roy Lasris, a Commonwealth of Virginia lawyer, and also former USAF JAG, who invented this remarkable document assembly application, Pathagoras. www.pathagoras.com

I have been using Pathagoras for several years to accelerate the production of accurate documents. Pathagoras scans the variable fields from a document template, name, date, address, etc., and creates a questionnaire for the interviewer to fill out during the interview process.

In fairness, Baron Henley, who is certified in the Nexis/Lexis Application HotDocs, can make that application perform wonders, but I have found Roy to be generous with his time, and perhaps be too generous with his support and tutorial materials. I did not find that to be the case with HotDocs, who, last time I checked, charged $800 for an all-day seminar in Ohio. I just learned that Lexis/Nexis has sold HotDocs to Capsoft and that it is marketed as being good for bank, insurance companies and big business. That confirms my strong feelings, but try it if you care to: https://www.hotdocs.com/press/capsoft-buys-hotdocs-software-business-lexisnexis

Pathagoras just happens to be the program I use. I think it is ideal for small firms, especially family law, particularly for cost and for the 90-day use of a full featured version. Purchasers get a one-hour online training session with Roy. My ulterior motive, if I have one, is to get a core of WV users, particularly in family law, so we can share templates, and modify and improve them, to the benefit of everyone including our clients.

These are some of my most useful articles:

This recent post is a two-page letter to my clients. They are required to read it and sign. It describes my way of doing things, my ethical standards, and stupid things they must avoid. https://wp.me/p4utce-13s .

This is a proposal I wrote, following the last WV State Bar Meeting, I proposed the Young Lawyers' Section do the appropriate homework and locate vendors for a turnkey technology system for small firms (Editor's note: as of this date, 03-15-2018, the specifics of this proposal need to be updated.)

http://hunterlawfirm.net/a-proposal-on-behalf-of-new-and-small-firm-wv-lawyers-a-turnkey-office-technology-system/

ORGANIZING THE FACTS IN YOUR CASE

The more I can empower my clients to gather and organize facts on their own, the more time and money I can save them. I will try to talk more about it later, but I strongly urge you to read "Digging down...." It is a three-legged stool: 1. The objects "puzzle pieces", the people, documents, and other things that form the puzzle picture; 2. "Top Ten Lists" Worries, goals, questions, gripes; and 3. The chronology, often put into a timeline exhibit.

That's the secret for small firm lawyer to prepare for that dispute or civil trial or mediation.

http://hunterlawfirm.net/digging-2018-short-sweet/

http://hunterlawfirm.net/2018-revised-digging-organizing-preparing-case/

10.   Social Media Marketing

The following is a rather robust summary of my efforts to market and express myself, and screenshots of various websites, reviews, and information resources published in Dec. 2014, and my first article on my efforts to obtain good reviews, published in August 2014. Again, I could just click to this site and use it as a course outline.

http://hunterlawfirm.net/social-media-annual-review-marketing-for-the-small-firm-lawyer/

http://hunterlawfirm.net/more-on-social-media-reviews-of-lawyers/

11.   The Family Court Restraining Order Act

The next article is an abrupt swerve. It is a summary of my experiences during the passage of WV Code 51-2A-2a. "Family court jurisdiction to restrict contact between parties," just as our Supreme Court was emasculating Family Courts from restraining all bad behavior except domestic violence. It has attracted very little attention, but I think it gives Courts an essential tool to moderate behavior that hurts parties, families, and children. It passed on the very day that the Supreme Court was taking to task small firm lawyer Jerry Blair of Clarksburg. I agreed with Mr. Blair. The Court did not.

The Court in Miller v. Riffle emasculated our Family Courts, and #51-2A-2a, un-emasculated them.

http://hunterlawfirm.net/the-wv-senate-bill-430-now-a-law-that-no-one-heard-of/

12.   Unbundling of Legal Services in Practice

I have been polishing a product to help the low-income client, and people who need some essential legal services but do not know how to go about finding them, or perhaps do not know they need them. A small flat fee covers a variety of services:

A.   http://hunterlawfirm.net/when-you-cant-or-wont-hire-a-lawyer-a-possible-option/

B.   http://hunterlawfirm.net/your-legal-checkup-and-
        review/

13.   Information and Task Management

Managing tasks and information are a constant challenge. I
think the key for the future is ease of use, over multiple
platforms. That means your tasks, calendar, contacts, and e-
mail. I talk here about Wunderlist, Evernote, and the on-line
training services www.Lynda.com and www.Udemy.com.
David Duffield of Duffield, Lovejoy and Stemple in
Huntington presented an application similar to Wunderlist
named "Todolist." Pick the one that suits you and "go for it"!
The key is prioritization; the "quick fixes," "urgent and now;"
and "not urgent but very important," all must be tended to in
their good time.

http://hunterlawfirm.net/a-wunderful-step-forward-in-my-
task-management/

http://hunterlawfirm.net/internet-learning-opportunities-
evernote-and-lynda-com/ , and www.udemy.com

14.   Law Practice Tips and Solutions

These are practical tips and solutions to several daily challenges
for lawyers, making sure you can prove mail was received,
dealing with non-communicative lawyers and parties, helping
process servers find the defendant, figuring out when your
client is lying, figuring how to prioritize your tasks, and several
more. My pick of 11 important sites include lawyers with great
"links" and government sites.

A.   http://hunterlawfirm.net/practical-tips-for-lawyers-8-
        14-2012/

B.   http://hunterlawfirm.net/the-lawyers-golden-rule-for-sheriffs-and-private-process-servers/

C.   http://hunterlawfirm.net/burts-lie-detector/

D.   http://hunterlawfirm.net/how-to-be-productive-while-preserving-ones-sanity/

E.   http://hunterlawfirm.net/burts-picks-of-11-important-websites/

15.   Family Law, Professionalism, and Collegiality

These are some family law posts, on lawyers who are not candid, four articles on alimony, WV's law of equitable distribution, "divorce 101," "the nuts and bolts of family court," and keeping in mind the sometimes-hidden interests impacting settlement discussions and mediation.

A.   http://hunterlawfirm.net/disingenuous-lawyers/

B.   http://hunterlawfirm.net/tag/perspectives-of-a-small-town-lawyer-2/page/15/

C.   http://hunterlawfirm.net/equitable-distribution-wv-divorce-property-law/

D.   http://hunterlawfirm.net/divorce-101-handout-october-5-2011/

E.   http://hunterlawfirm.net/the-nuts-and-bolts-of-family-court/

F.   http://hunterlawfirm.net/lessons-from-hatfields-mccoys/

G.   http://hunterlawfirm.net/family-law-practice-tip-equitable-distribution-and-alimony-spreadsheets/

BURTON'S VIEWS OF THE WORLD

These are some of my favorite posts, on my view of the world and our place in it:

A.   http://hunterlawfirm.net/burts-criticism-of-religion-and-religiosity/

B.   http://hunterlawfirm.net/burts-response-to-the-challenges-of-the-modern-world/

C.   http://hunterlawfirm.net/obesity-and-the-law-and-how-not-to-be-fat/

D.   http://hunterlawfirm.net/some-thoughts-on-hunting-for-trophy-animals-and-some-tips-on-punctuation/

E.   http://hunterlawfirm.net/a-life-of-reading/

F.   http://hunterlawfirm.net/a-small-town-lawyers-reading-list/

PERSONAL INJURY POSTS:

My personal injury posts are generally designed to dispel misconceptions and educate the potential client

A.   http://hunterlawfirm.net/personal-injury-client-misperceptions/

B.   http://hunterlawfirm.net/dear-personal-injury-client-points-to-remember/

C.   http://hunterlawfirm.net/not-the-normal-personal-injury-blah-blah/

D.   http://hunterlawfirm.net/the-chinese-curse-may-you-have-a-mild-closed-head-injury-and-what-if-it-happens-to-you/

E.   http://hunterlawfirm.net/various-insurance-coverages/

F.   http://hunterlawfirm.net/what-sue-my-employer-deliberate-intent/

Mediation: a search that produced 73 (Now 97) results for "mediation." I passionately believe in mediation, and lots of thoughts on the subject. Some of my opinions are against the mainstream:

http://hunterlawfirm.net/?s=Mediation

With a practice that includes family law, personal injury, civil, and mediation, I have had plenty of opportunity to see huge differences in mediation depending on the parties, issues, and forum. A good lawyer will master the differences.

http://hunterlawfirm.net/a-foot-in-each-camp/

As new lawyers appear in Buckhannon, I have tried to mentor them with my views on "hanging out your shingle." Truly not for the faint of heart!

http://hunterlawfirm.net/hanging-out-your-shingle-not-for-the-faint-of-heart/

SOCIAL MEDIA MARKETING

Google Search yourself:

https://www.google.com/#q=J.+Burton+Hunter+III

Does your site invite visitors to read your reviews?

http://hunterlawfirm.net/our-reviews/

Raise your score from 6.5 to 10.0 Avvo.com

http://www.avvo.com/attorneys/26201-wv-j-hunter-4508877.html

Here is my Google+ Home Page:

https://plus.google.com/108608274932908874385/about

Justia Lawyers "Compare 53 Lawyers Serving Buckhannon, WV"

https://www.justia.com/lawyers/west-virginia/buckhannon

Check your profile page on Justia. Is it professional?

https://lawyers.justia.com/lawyer/mr-j-burton-hunter-iii-1497838

https://lawyers.justia.com/lawyer/mr-j-burton-hunter-iii-1497838

www.findlaw.com and Burton Hunter:

http://pview.findlaw.com/view/2443583_1

Even one bad review can drag you down: "Incompetent at Best - This guy is an overpriced arrogant jerk." by jaynajane

http://www.merchantcircle.com/business/J.Burton.Hunter.III.and.Associates.PLLC.304-472-7477/review/list#reviews

YEXT: My son John advises:

"More in depth local directory monitoring tool. Be more cautious with this one as they request a phone number and are more aggressive with marketing the 'enhanced services'."

This is the one I have just subscribed to for two years. It starts with a 45 minute training session. You fill out YEXT's master form and it checks the sites you have already claimed and conforms your information, and then it syncs your master form to the remaining of 60 sites.

http://www.yext.com/

I include the listings below so you can see the 60 sites that YEXT will synch you to:

NPR is promoting this site, which covers "The New News," Ozymandias, "Ozy" for short

Trends, discoveries, technology, modernity. http://www.ozy.com/

16. Document Assembly for the Busy Non-Nerdy Lawyer: Pathagoras

This article is targeted to other lawyers, particularly family law, but it also gives insights to potential clients, or even judges, of how our office produces so much so quickly.

I am writing about the "document assembly" application Pathagoras. It is available as a free, full featured, 90 day trial download: [2]www.pathagoras.com

Caveat: the "master list" form that I describe as a work in progress is just that. I don't yet trust it to use as the portal for all of my forms. Safest is to use the form, save the data, and slowly build, using that as a source for the other forms, or using it to start the master form. I will keep working with the hope that one "master list" will contain data for use in every one of the client's family case documents. Stay tuned!

A.   I own no share in the company, and this is not a commercial, but I have a stake in spreading Pathagoras.

B.   WV lawyers, and the family law bar especially, need this product. It needs dozens, or hundreds, of WV family lawyers to create and share forms and templates.

C.   It needs lawyers to be able to fly through the paperwork, to crank out petitions, motions, emergency pleadings, parenting plans, property settlement agreements, cover letters, and permanent and temporary orders.

Note these features:

A.   A new questionnaire will appear. You could fill it in, but you already have Sallie's "master file"!

B.   Hit "scan," and it will look for the labels within the brackets: Pathagoras will ask you if you want to use a stored data file. Say "Yes!"

C.   Just go to the dropdown button, and there is Sallie Mae's master data file. You or your staff typed it in the very first time you met her.

D.   Select it, and Sallie's divorce petition and motion for temporary relief will fill in automatically!

E.   Select the optional paragraphs to keep and omit. Optional paragraphs are stored within "squiggly brackets," { _ _ _ _ _ _ _ }. Just select the ones appropriate to Sallie, the divorce grounds, whether she wants alimony, etc.

F.   Answer any remaining questions, and process the form by clicking "next."

G.   Your Petition and temporary motion, CCIS cover sheet, notice of hearing, and other documents will be created, subject to minor clean-up by your clerical staff.

H.   Later, you can do the same with your client's proposed parenting plan or property settlement agreement, the notices of hearings, the emergency motions, temporary and final orders, everything!

I.   Think how many time your staff types "Sallie Mae Smith" and "Billie Ray Smith;" dozens! They, and all the variable information, are already there!

J.   It is that simple.

K.   I caution you, my only criticism of Roy, which is really an admitted failure of my own, is that the program is so powerful that there are too many ways to do each function. I am smart, but I am not a programmer.

L.   For your day to day, bread and butter, document assembly, you don't have to learn that other stuff, but it is nice to know it's there, and as you get better, you will get braver.

M.   But, for now, just show me how to do it, and don't confuse me with alternate methods.

N.   For guidance, I suggest you start with "the basics": [4]https://www.pathagoras.com/help/Pathagoras %20 %27No %20Setup %27.pdf

O.   "Pathagorize" your first form, and create a document. You should then be hooked!

P.   Then, I urge you to do Roy's "7 Day Plan," but do it in two hours one afternoon, or you'll never get back to it: [5]https://www.pathagoras.com/help/Pathagoras %207day %20Plan.pdf

Q.   I am embarrassed to admit that I have trouble with online, detailed, manuals, such as Roy's 600-page comprehensive manual. Rather than read it through, I suggest liberal use of the table of contents and search engine.

R.   Then call me, or write, and I will send our dozen best forms. And you will be on your way, with a jump start I never had.

S.   If you buy the product, Roy will give you a 40 minute online and telephone tutorial.

T.   It is that simple. If you are as smart as I think you are, you will find dozens of uses for Pathagoras and will have an office policy that all documents you produce need to be Pathagorized. And you and I will be in a select group, sharing, collaborating, and helping one another and our clients. It will be a revolution in the practice of law.

One more thing about Pathagoras. It is simpler and cheaper than the alternatives.

17.   A Pathagoras Refresher

DEAR COLLEAGUES;

(and Burt's staff, friends, and family, since this software benefits <u>anyone</u> who needs to produce, assemble and distribute documents; feel free to forward to anyone whose business produces lots of documents.)

I am beginning my annual Pathagoras binge where I review the basics, reorganize my favorite forms/templates, and try to move forward on my goal to improve and streamline my document assembly. I was able to notify founder Roy Lasris that the link to one of his basic manuals, my favorite, had failed. Thanks for restoring it Roy. I also mentioned to him that the learning site www.Lynda.com has some great courses on popular applications for a monthly subscription price. Roy responded (he always responds positively to suggestions, even when he respectfully disagrees) that he will prepare some similar, but free, tutorial videos to supplement the ones below. Roy continues to be the most responsive, and responsible, software publisher I have ever encountered. Try contacting Microsoft or Nuance in case you doubt me. Below I have copied and pasted the Links to the Pathagoras manuals, tutorials, reviews, the free trial download, and purchasing and ordering information. Enjoy. I get no "kick-back," but please feel free to tell Roy, "Burt sent me!" I still look forward to the time that colleagues and I can share, refine, and invent a complete line of WV practice Pathagorized Word Forms! And don't forget Baron Henley's reminder that if you do not understand Word paragraph numbering, styles, and themes, you are NOT properly using Word.

Regards,

Burt

Pathagoras Document Assembly (Microsoft Word Based – No Programming Required) RESOURCES:

Beginner's Guide:

http://www.pathagoras.com/help/Pathagoras%20Beginners.pdf(Burt's favorite)

Basic:
http://www.pathagoras.com/help/Pathagoras%20%27No%20Setup%27.pdf

Seven Day Plan: (15 minutes per day):

http://www.pathagoras.com/help/Pathagoras%207day%20Plan.pdf(The second essential)

Pathagoras 600 Page Manual:

http://www.pathagoras.com/help/Pathagoras.pdf

Video Tutorials:

http://www.pathagoras.com/video.html

Free 90 Day Trial Pathagoras:

http://www.pathagoras.com/orderdemo.html

Reviews and Kudos:

http://www.pathagoras.com/reviews.html

Pricing and Order:

http://www.pathagoras.com/pricing.html

18.   My Legal Coach – My Lawyer?

Is this a trick question? Not really, but there is a difference. Let's say you have a divorce or custody case, or, that you, or you and your estranged partner, just want some guidance and help in getting through your legal problem.

Repeat after me: "You should not be your own lawyer if you can possibly afford to hire a lawyer to represent you!"

If you've read any of my stuff, you know that's a theme I harp on. But, I recognize that some people simply cannot afford "record counsel," and some are skeptical or even a tad arrogant or ignorant of the perils of self-representation. I have a product for these folks.

I call this type of product "unbundling of legal services." Not everyone can do this, but with my 46 years of experience I have posted 350 blog articles, over 1200 pages. Many of them constitute tutorials or templates for things every litigant should know.

Often there is a component of "ghost writing." A proposed parenting plan, property settlement agreement, final order, or petition or counter-petition is not that hard to do. A ghost writer can do them "on the cheap" if the author is not also becoming your record counsel. It is not representation, but it helps you "ante up," like in poker. The "Family Court Rules" require the filing of certain key documents. Your "coach" can help make sure they are "up to snuff."

We try to give the party who just can't afford any more than $500 at least $1000 worth of information and training in "the rules of the game." I accept a reasonable number of follow up calls, and, so long as you haven't screwed up your case too badly, I will often remain available to be retained.

For the skeptic, I try to show the risk benefit of hiring me for full representation. Perhaps 50% of such clients eventually hire me, getting credit for the first $500 payment. And, for those who do not, it's the same rule. I may be willing to take on the representation if you have not screwed it up too badly. Warning, the old quoted retainer may no longer be possible.

We have handouts about how to involve the other party in the lives of the children while looking good to the court, how to enforce your agreement, and how to negotiate a divorce settlement. We have informational articles on equitable distribution, alimony, custody, retirement benefits, essential insurance coverages, a "legal check-up," mediation, and myriad other topics.

19. Self-Represented Mediation

While no lawyer can represent both sides, a trained and experienced mediator can meet with both parties and draft a variety of documents, agreements, parenting plans, and even pleadings. He/she must meet ethical standards, but for parties who have differences but not severe dysfunction, this low-cost option at least allows you a full veto, which a contested hearing does not. There is no agreement unless BOTH parties to mediation sign on.

The concept again is "unbundling of legal services." It is a way to get quick results, if not perfectly tailored, while keeping many options open if things turn nasty. Please call me at 304-472-7477, or write, hunterjb@hunterlawfirm.net, if you have any questions!

20. The Lost Art of the Letter: and Finding a Perfect Informal Font

Susan Jacoby's "The Age of American Unreason" https://tinyurl.com/yasc7trz , is a brilliant assessment of the last 50 years of American Intellectual thought, but:

A.   It was published in Feb. 2008, which means it missed the smart phone and Donald Trump!

B.   She ends it in a bit of a rant about the relative uselessness of the screen, decries the death of reading of traditional books, and by attacking Wikipedia and espousing a return to "original sources" for research, ignored that she had no way of knowing where we would be in 10-15 or 20 years. She also disdains the 99% of us, some of who have something to say but not the time to return to physical libraries, especially in faraway places.

C.   In my life, I can find a definition, a term, a fact, a news story, a podcast, a book, the weather, directions, music, or an app, with a simple voice command. And, remember, even in the summer of 2018, "We're just gittin' started!"

D.   Then I found an article in Joanna Gains' "Magnolia Journal" on the lost art of letter writing. What the author missed, for me, is that my handwriting is terrible, worse now that fingers are crabbing into permanent keyboarding devices.

E.   I will miss e-mail if it goes. Text is so brief, ridiculous in its abbreviations, and best used as evidence in nasty custody fights.

F.   As you can see here, I tend to break the rule that paragraphs should be longer than a sentence. Screens are easier to read if the writing is clear and concise.

G.   I have this thing I call a "substantive e-mail". I can still dictate a formal letter, but for copying several people, my family, multiple counsel, my staff, and clients, or my fraternity brothers or Linsly Military School high

205

school classmates, a well written e-mail can be invaluable.

H.   So, I am going to try to evolve my e-mail and digital writing. More concise, as I tend to ramble, but not evanescent. (A word Siri just looked up for me!)

I.   So, this morning I checked the fonts in Word 16, and searched Google for a couple more, and they are below. I want a replacement, that my distant cousin Gage, from Tasmania, who was not taught "cursive", can read.

J.   Here is what I found? What do you think?

Harlow Solid Italic: This is a test of this new font which I do not like.

Brush Script: This is good old brush script, which I always have to increase font size and bold to make usable.

Comic Sans: Up to now, Comic Sans has been my favorite font for a personal letter, often in **bold**. |

Black Adder ITC is just too busy for me.

English 157 BT is too fine and too cursive!

Forte seems a bit too bold! But better unbolded.

Freehand 521 BJ seems to be a candidate, but not for my cramped, backslanted handwriting.

Harlow Solid Italic make me think of fluorescent lights at a drive in restaurant.

Lucinda handwriting; another candidate, but too feminine.

Sego print; pretty neat; **perhaps if it is bolded?**

Segoe script; too cute, **but also perhaps better bolded?**

Vladimir Script no way! Not even if bolded and increased in size!

Vic Modern Cursive: a bit feminine but per haps in bold?

K.

L.   As I spend this week with our grandchildren, ages 13 and 9, I am seeing how they use screens.

M.   Our nine-year-old grandson loves crossword puzzles, although he looks up the answers and fills in the blanks.

N.   Last night he was intensely viewing his grandmother's iPhone. Turns out he was watching short tutorials including "How to Organize Yourself". Who knew!?

O.   Almost every student we saw, going to and from school and practice, was looking at a screen. But they weren't alone.

P.   I am directly aware the horrors that lurk here, bullying, loss of privacy, distraction. But that is a big subject of its own.

Q.   These kids were in touch with family and friends. I realized that our granddaughter was in regular touch with her Mom, who is with Daddy on a well deserved vacation to a Caribbean Island. No more waiting by the phone hoping for a "long distance phone call."

R.   Just like we wasted time on comic books, situation comedies, and The Hardy Boys, modern parents must learn new skills to guide the young to worthwhile sources, but we can't push the world back to Gutenberg or Papyrus!

S.   We are on the "accelerating change train/spaceship" and we had best learn to enjoy the ride!

So, which font do you want me to write you with?

VII.
THOUGHTS OF THE WORLD, PHILOSOPHY, POLITICS, AND *STUFF*

1.   Burton Hunter's View of the World

A Small-Town Lawyer's Reading List #1

Since September 2016, I have read or dabbled in many books, biographies, memoir, a few novels, and books on rationality, philosophy, religion, and accelerating change. In a time when America seems to be going haywire, where political and religious partisans rule the day, and where people seem no longer to seek out and find common ground, good reading, for as many of us as possible, is a desirable goal. It will not tell you how to prosecute your divorce or resolve your dispute, but my list has many excellent books, and it is a small window into this lawyer, should you decide to hire him or read his stuff.

These books are in no particular order and are not arranged by topics. All are reviewed in Amazon:

A.   No Ordinary Time: Franklin and Eleanor Roosevelt. The Home Front in WW II, Doris Kearns Goodwin

B.   Sapiens – A Brief History of HUMANKIND: Yoval Noah Harari

C.   Homo Deus – A Brief History of the Future: Yoval Hoah Harari

D.   Sourdough: A Novel: Robin Sloan

E.   Leonardo da Vinci: Walter Isaacson

F.   Einstein: Walter Isaacson

G.   The Undoing Project – A Friendship That Changed Our Minds: Michael Lewis

H.   A Woman in Charge – The Life of Hillary Rodham Clinton

I.   The Age of American Unreason: Susan Jacoby

J.   American Ulysses: A Life of Ulysses S. Grant: Ronald C. White, Jr.

K.   The Origins of Totalitarianism: Hannah Arendt

L.   Fantasyland: How America Went Haywire, a 500 History: Kurt Anderson

M.   Transition – A Mental Autobiography: Will Durant

N.   Dr. Gundry's Diet Evolution: Steven R. Gundry, M.D.

O.   John Wesley – A Biography: Stephen Tomkins

P.   The Book – A Cover-To-Cover Exploration of the Most Powerful Object of Our Time: Keith Houston

Q.   Thomas Wolfe – A Biography: Elizabeth Nowell

R.   A. Lincoln – A Biography: Ronald C. White, Jr.

S.   Island of the World - A Novel: Michael D. O'Brien

T.   James Madison and the Making of America: Kevin R.C. Gutzman

U.   Naked: David Sedaris

V.   The River of Doubt – Theodore Roosevelt's Darkest Journey: Candice Millard

W.   One L: Scott Turow

X.   The Essential Social Media Handbook: Gail Z. Martin

Y.   The Divinity of Doubt: God and Atheism on Trial: Vincent Bugliosi

Z.   The Princes of Ireland – The Dublin Saga: Edward Rutherford

AA.   The Storm Before the Storm – The Beginning of the End of the Roman Republic: Mike Duncan

BB.   Goethe – Life as Work of Art: Rudiger Safranski

CC.   The Art of Memoir: Mary Karr

DD.   Ad Infinitum – A Biography of Latin: Nicholas Ostler

EE.   Constantine's Sword – The Church and the Jews: James Carroll

FF.   Salman Rushde – A Memoir: Joseph Anton

GG.   Andrew Carnegie: David Nasaw

HH.   A Troublesome Inheritance – Genes, Race, and Human History: Nicholas Wade

II.   Fire and Fury: Inside the Trump White House: Michael Wolff

JJ.   The Information – a History, a Theory, a Flood: James Gleick

KK.   A Book Forged in Hell: Spinoza's Scandalous Treatise and the Birth of the Secular Age: Steven Nadler

LL.   A Universe From Nothing: Why There is Something Rather Than Nothing: Lawrence M. Kraus

MM.   The Meaning of Human Existence: Edward O. Wilson

NN.   Maphead – Charting the Wide, Weird World of Maps: Ken Jennings

I started to compile a list of books that I have used, over the last ten years or so, as the foundation of my understanding of the modern world. It is more a bibliography than anything that a particular lawyer needs to read on a particular day.

I have mentioned some of these books in prior postings, and they definitely are with me when I write anything. Some are easier reads than others, but they are solid writings, by Pulitzer Prize and Nobel prize winners. All that are rated on Amazon are four stars or better. Here they are:

Reading list:

A.   <u>Night,</u> by Elie Weisel; 120 pages by the Winner of the Nobel Peace Prize. "A slim volume of terrible power." New York Times.

B. Future Shock; by Alvin Toffler; a must for anyone wanting to understand the modern world; $01 used at Amazon; $.99 from Kindle;

C. Anything by Asimov, Heinlein, Silverburg, Clark, etc. They gave me perspective

D. What Technology Wants: Kevin Kelley (The formula? 60% of new technology is positive, and 40% is negative. That comports with my experience.)

E. The Courtier and the Heretic: Leibniz, Spinoza, and the Fate of God in the Modern World; Matthew Stewart

F. The Clockwork Universe, Isaac Newton, the Royal Society, and the Birth of the Modern World

G. The Song of the Dodo: Island Bio-geography in an Age of Extinctions by David Quammen

H. Collapse: How Societies Choose to Fail or Succeed: Revised Edition; Jared Diamond

I. Guns, Germs, and Steel, Jared Diamond

J. The End of Lawyers, Rethinking the Nature of Legal Services, Richard Susskind (boring, boring, boring! I do not see this impacting our world in WV, except on short term such as "LegalZoom.com.")

K. The Social Media Bible, Tactics, Tools & Strategies for Business Success, Lon Safko and David K. Brake. (My version is 2009; new version May, 2012; very comprehensive, 800 pages, but not a "how to" book.

L.   The Myth of the Paperless Office, Abegail J. Sellen and Richard H.R. Harper (2003, also outdated, but it defines the challenge. The basic premise, "paper-less," remains true.")

M.   Scrolling Forward, David M. Levy, also outdated 2001, but a favorite of mine. Contains a history of the document.

N.   Thinking Fast and Slow; Daniel Kahneman; a tough read by a Nobel Prize winning economist/mathematician on how our thinking tends not to comport with reality.

O.   The Map that Changed the World; William Smith and the Birth of Modern Geology; (The creator and creation of the first geological map of Great Britain.)

P.   The Beak of the Finch: A Story of Evolution in Our Time; Jonathan Weiner: a great little primer on evolution, and how it works in our time.

Q.   How the Scots Invented the Modern World: "The True Story of How Western Europe's Poorest Nation Created Our World & Everything in It," by Arthur Herman.

R.   Small Pieces Loosely Joined; "A Unified Theory of the Web," by David Weinberger. 2002. It helped me get a handle of this amazing thing, "The World Wide Web."

S.   Defenders of the Faith, "Christianity and Islam Battle For the Soul of Europe (Suliman and Charles V, Henry the VIIIth and Pope Clement), by James Reston, Jr. A gift from my wife Nancy. Some roots of the conflict of Islam, Christianity, and the world.

T.	Bird by Bird, by Ann Lamott; a great little book; "Some Instructions on Writing and Life."

U.	Effective Time Management; by Lothar Seiwert and Holger Woeltje. A good tutorial and reminder of office time management based on Microsoft Outlook.

V.	Edwin Newman on Language, Strictly Speaking and A Civil Tongue; Old school but great stuff; no "hopefully" or "healthy food."

W.	The Metaphysical Club, A Story of Ideas in America, by Louis Menand, Winner of the Pulitzer Prize. The story of the American thinkers Ralph Waldo Emerson, William James, Oliver Wendell Holmes Jr., John Dewey, and many other American thinkers of the 19th century.

If this isn't enough, controversial writings of the anti-religionists (atheists/skeptics), Sam Harris, Christopher Hitchens, and Richard Dawkins argue, a tad arrogantly, for rational thought and against superstition, and are always entertaining, and the books of Malcolm Gladwell, such as The Tipping Point, Blink, and Outliers, are thought provoking but not necessarily scientifically confirmed.

Anything by Bill Bryson is entertaining and informative, especially "A Short History of Nearly Everything."

Finally, for a whopping big novel, Charles Dickens' Bleak House. Also, The Checklist Manifesto, which makes the case for checklists in nearly any human endeavor, and the story of cancer, <u>The Emperor of Maladies</u>. I could go on, and probably will. Happy reading.

2. Global Warming: How the Environmental Movement Has Botched It!

This is my "take" on the environmental movement and its emphasis on "Global Warming." To me that approach is self-defeating.

I read a lot of things that touch on environmentalism but are not so labeled. I follow the news carefully but greatly miss my weekly Time and Newsweek which helped give me perspective. Nevertheless, I average approximately two hours of news per day and another hour or two of reading. These are my pleasures, so somehow, I fit   them in.

I believe the environmental movement has "blown it," and I wonder who decided to focus so much on global warming. In retrospect, I believe it is the wrong approach.

Jane Goodall, Jacques Cousteau, David Quammem in his great classic on speciation, "The Song of the Dodo, Rachel Carson in "Silent Spring," Richard Attenborough in "Planet Earth," the Disney documentaries and movies, Harari's "Sapiens," and so many other sources have revealed the great destruction of the species of the world, of   the great forests and rivers, and the huge explosion of resource-consuming human beings and their domesticated animals whose combined weight equals 75 % of all living creatures. Poisons and processed sugary foods are killing   us slowly, but by the millions. Tribalism and "political famines" cause mass human misery.

This "human pestilence" has absorbed the resources of the world, spewing out pollution, and putting toxic poisons in everything we breathe and drink.

The story of the poisoning of our planet and depletion of our resources is a powerful one, and relatively easy to prove by the scientific method. But, instead of focusing on the things people can see and feel, the environmentalists decided to hitch their wagon to "global warming."

Yes, it is a concern that Upshur County, WV might become as hot as Fort Mill SC in the summer, and that our native animals may have to move north, and that we may get our share of fire ants and other southern critters.

There is no doubt the heating of the earth is terribly serious, the rising of the oceans, the shrinking of our glaciers, and the unforeseen consequences. But it seems to be hard for people to wrap their head around.

However, the number of species in the world is countable; the amount of poison in the air is measurable; the history of failed civilizations such as the Mayans and Easter Island is available to us, and there is so much that science can reveal right here, in our immediate present and future, to help galvanize America and humankind to action.

Instead, the environmental movement gives the polluters and the conservative right a tool to continue to deny the truth in order to protect their short-term profits and line their pockets with gold. Donald Trump can say that global warming is a conspiracy developed to benefit the Chinese, and people will vote for him in droves. He can campaign and tell people not to worry, that it is all a hoax and that he will bring coal jobs back, and even traditional conservatives will back him, from perceived self-interest, and because "Global Warning" is so darn hard to prove.

If "they put me in charge," we would immediately change to:

A.   We are being poisoned;

B.   We are pushing other living creatures to the fringes, creatures who are the source of the wonder in our world and are potential resources that are incalculable for our well-being.

C.   That there are things we can do to slow and stop the great extinction of species.

D.   We are allowing the sun to come through our atmosphere and cause cancer in us and our children, and if we don't do something about it, civilization could fall apart.

E.   I would focus on the poisoning and then move to the symptoms. Al Gore spoke of treating our atmosphere as a place to dump raw sewage. Now that's an analogy people can picture.

F.   I would move the fact that the earth is getting warmer to a secondary position, as a symptom and not the cause, but one that can eventually tip the scales towards putting us out of business!

G.   I would stress the need for space science! Yep; with all our eggs in one basket, our species is as fragile as a flower; spread to other planets and even solar systems gives us a fighting chance to become what we are capable of evolving to.

H.   That's just me, but we all get to put in our "two cents."

http://hunterlawfirm.net/wp-content/uploads/2017/06/6.2.1.2017.jpg

3.   Burton's Challenge to the Church in the Modern World

I have been struggling with the fact that my church, The United Methodist, is dying. Quite literally, its members are dying and not being replaced with equal numbers.

The reasons are complex, but the most obvious is its assertion of the supernatural as fact. The "magic word" of course is "Faith." That is supposed to excuse all the silliness.

Jesus, who the church assumes really existed in flesh and blood, and maybe he did, is somehow equal to, or is, God.

As I have written before in Perspectives of a Small-Town Lawyer, each religion seems unable to resist giving its founder supernatural trappings and attempting to control the thinking of its penitents.

I cannot tolerate this, but I remain in the church, where I have been, with some interruptions for 72 years.

Almost as obvious to me is that the church requires this "faith" of its members. If you don't have it, they don't really want you. I make my way in the church by keeping these views to myself, and attending choir and church, and participating. I avoid Sunday school and discussion groups.

While I agree with Prof. Richard Dawkins in his reliance on the truths that science provides, I am resisting his assertions that skeptics need to unite and outcompete religion. Militant atheists sound to me no different than other closed-minded groups.

For now, I shall not become a "group of one," but will try to suggest a way my religion can become tolerable to me and survive in the modern world. I confess, I do not think it can.

For purposes of this analysis, I will pretend the world had four kinds of people, and myself (a fifth group composed of one person).

Group 1: People who are limited by tradition, learning, intelligence, fear, or delusion and who believe in supernatural religious concepts such as heaven, hell, and myth as truth.

Group 2: People who know in their hearts that the supernatural does not exist (except that certain clothes, words, or rituals effect the outcome of sports contests), but because of tradition, fear, or a desire not to offend act as if they believe and feel ambivalence.

Group 3: Intelligent, well educated people who acknowledge that the supernatural doesn't exist but who want their church to survive and want to believe, at the very least, that something intelligent got things going and set up the order of things.

Group 4: Hard-headed, assertive, and sometimes militant, believers in science who are willing to call themselves atheists and are strongly anti-religion.

Then there is I, who do not believe in the supernatural, or a sentient creator (prime mover), but who expects never to accept a label like atheist or even agnostic. My group of one does not wish for the end of all religion (yet, but I have certainly been considering it) because no one has figured out what will replace it. I at least want to have an idea before I chuck the whole thing. Also, for now, I wish to remain a member of the church I have been with for a lifetime.

Flash back 52 years or so to a Methodist Youth Fellowship (M.Y.F.) regional gathering at the Moundsville, WV, Methodist Church in Marshall County. Our speaker was a good-looking college basketball player, all conference point guard from a Va. small college. He had been "saved" and wanted the same fate for us. He told of his conversion and his desire to serve the Lord via Jesus. I felt - nothing. It made me uncomfortable.

At the end of his sermon, he announced the organist was going to play hymns in order to give us time to feel the spirit, come to the alter-rail, kneel, and be saved. Some of the kids were crying, others were clearly moved, and most appeared embarrassed to stay in their pews. And then there were the few of us who refused to budge.

Some hopped up happily and came up to kneel. I figured they were pretty much saved already. Others slowly followed, and I was surprised that some simply caved to the pressure and reluctantly knelt. That's when I knew I would never be saved. But flash back, and forward, again:

A.   When I was perhaps five, maybe six, I got my cousin Karen to confirm what I had figured out by counting the chimneys in my grandparents' neighborhood and multiplying (although I knew not what that was) them by the dozens of other neighborhoods that existed in the world, that there was no Santa Claus. Reluctantly, cousin Karen filled in for me the mystery of the toys under the tree, and got in trouble.

B.　　But, as an adult, when a close family member was facing permanent disability or death, I promised something unknown and unseen that if that person were restored to health, I would sing in our choir to the day my breath ran out. As I sit here, I love singing in the choir, but I stay there, and in the church, hypocrite or not, because I dare not go back on that promise. You see, that person was not just restored to health but was set on a path to an exemplary and happy and productive life. Who can argue with that.

Where am I headed with this? To the question how does one reconcile a belief that religion is based on fear and ignorance, control and prejudice, and that its time has come, with a belief that mankind needs every source of ethics and morality it can use?

For myself, and other skeptics, how does a person who does not believe the teachings of the supernatural presented at every sermon and Sunday school justify spending a few hours each week at a church service or choir practice?

I have given my word on two profound things in my life:

A.　　If Nancy would fall in love with and marry me, I would try to be a good husband and father; and,

B.　　If a close relative would recover from a life-threatening illness, I would stay in the choir, and therefore the church, for life.

Since writing the paragraphs above, I have watched the movie "Noah," one of the worst movies I have ever seen, and received a review of "God is Not Dead" from a person I respect who says it catered to every prejudice and fear of the religious right. He says the only thing it lacked was Ted Nugent cutting off the heads of unbelievers.

Noah was one of the silliest and worst movies I ever saw.

This paragraph is the transition paragraphs for two articles I have written. Above I discuss how I have got to this point in my thinking, and below separate the teachings in the Bible (Old and New Testaments) in unimportant and important.

My conclusion is there is nothing in the Bible regarding the supernatural that needs to be there in a modern world. If you have the patience, read on and see if you believe me.

REMEMBER: IMPORTANT VS. UNIMPORTANT!

U = Unimportant

I = Important

U - Everything was created by an infinitely wise and powerful creator or prime mover.

I - Something existed that turned into our universe. There is no evidence that this "something" was a creator or was created by a creator. Our universe just might be one of an infinite number of universes, and there is certainly nothing "special" about our solar system or us.

U - That the world was created in seven days, and then God rested.

I - That the best evidence supports an inconceivably vast explosion from a tiny dense "singularity," the size of a walnut, 13 billion years ago. And that 300,000 years later the material dispersed began to coalesce into galaxies of stars, many of which gained orbiting planets.

U - That all species of creatures were created by God at the same time, were immutable, exist now as they always have, and have only existed for 5000 years or so.

I - That although the exact mechanism remains a mystery, the phenomenon we call "life" began on earth with the right combination of moisture, material, and temperature around 3.6 billion years ago. Since there seems to be nothing special about earth, life probably exists elsewhere in the universe.

U - That a vengeful, and rather infantile, God (all powerful, but for some reason allowing things to spin out of control), became angry at mankind for straying from his wishes, especially the descendants of Cain, decided to commit genocide, regardless of individual justice, and select just a few favorites as well of 2 of each species of animal and plant, so the world could have a "fresh start" and so things could be perfect thereafter.

I. This story ignores so many scientific fundamentals that to believe it would require a person to believe multiple, exclusive, opposing views at once. A few such conflicts are the millions of species that would have to be loaded on the relatively small ark, that Noah and his family were helped by fallen supernatural beings called angels, that any species reduced only to members would almost certainly go extinct, and that Adam's and Eve's descendants would have to engage in endless incest.

U - That species that God "created" cannot change.

I - As occasional mutations in cells occurred, some of those mutations resulted in organizations of cells better able to survive and reproduce. This "natural selection" inexorably caused life to "evolve" with what in retrospect appears to "common sense" to have been created by an intelligent being.

U - That God created Adam in his own image from dust and breathed life into him, and then put Adam under an ethereal anesthetic and created Eve from Adam's Rib.

I - That creatures which evolved in the sea left the sea, and that a branch of that life form stopped laying eggs and began feeding its young with a product of the mother's body, milk, allowing slower growth time and a species with a larger brain that eventually developed opposable finger and thumb and a form of self-awareness that exceeds all other species.

U - That the woman, Eve, hooked up with evil incarnate, Satan in the form of a serpent, to eat a special throbbing (according to Russell Crowe) red fruit, tempting Adam with it and getting them kicked out of the Garden of Eden. (Leaving out any explanation of how, then or after the Great Flood of Noah, how a pair of any species could multiply into millions and billions.)

I - That when mankind did not know something, such as how it came to be, how the earth was formed, or why natural events such as earthquakes, plagues, floods, or powerful storms occur, members of the family or tribe simply made up or hallucinated the answer. Groups of "believers" organized into religions with leaders who had special insights into the truth justifying the imposition of these beliefs, based on "faith," upon others.

I - There existed on the earth a particularly deep and wide landmass (Eurasia) that evolved a greater complexity and number of species than other areas, such as North and South America or Australia. Civilization was born there because of

224

Mankind's ability to domesticate animals and plants, and to spread because of its greater sophistication and the germs that evolved in its many animal species.

U - God gave certain prophets "the inside story" who communicated "the truth" to others. One prophecy was the birth of a savior who would "save" mankind.

U - According to Christian religion, God sent an angel to an unwed woman to tell her she would become pregnant without sex, and got a fellow named Joseph to accept this as true and marry the woman and help raise her child.

I and U - That as culture matured from being nomadic, tribal, and territorial, the concept of empathy and mercy emerged. Apparently, a person or small group of persons put together a list of "do's and don'ts," built upon The Ten Commandments and "The Golden Rule" to guide people in their behavior and ostensibly to set them up to live in a spiritual world of perfection for eternity. Unfortunately, as Adam, Noah, Mohamed, and Jesus would be sad to know, there has been a lot of backsliding going on.

U - Certain groups figured out "the truth," and other groups were heretics or non-believers who the true believers were entitled to persecute, ostracize, mutilate, and kill.

I - Every religious group, especially a rather arrogant one that calls itself "Atheism," is certain that its "can't-helps" are true and that even small deviations from the group's precepts are going to lead others into serious problems, including but not limited to, burning eternally in the fire and brimstone of hell. But no single group has all the answers.

U - Questions such as whether Jesus was man, God or man and God at the same time, or whether there is something called "the holy spirit" are profoundly important.

I - Questions such as the ones above are ridiculous and divisive.

U - The most intense, aggressive, and devout group, say militant Islam, should and will prevail, until all the people of the world will be subordinate to the teachings of Mohammed and his laws.

U - Even the Moslems can't agree among themselves, and the Sunni's and the Shiites enjoy killing one another as much as they do Christians. And for 1100 years in Byzantium, Christians killed millions over the nature of Jesus or whether they should venerate (worship) objects.

I - The most rational of human beings accept the scientific method as the best method ever devised to reach objective truth. That rational and secular approach seems the least likely to end in the destruction of mankind by word or natural event. Even the most tolerant of religions looks down on anyone who does not accept that religion's precepts on faith. And virtually every religion demands you accept its guy as having supernatural powers or insights.

U - The best way for religion (say the Christian Faith) to survive is to hunker down, return to its fundamentalist roots, and rage against social change.

I - The only sane religion must be one tolerant of other beliefs, rational, open to most anyone, and focused on core ideas that encourage curiosity, individual thought, the methods of science, and our simple, physical, survival.

226

I - Focusing on United Methodism, a traditional, mainstream, non-radical arm of Christianity, I believe that it should be just as happy that a rational non-believer wants to be a member, as a blind follower; more actually, since the rational non-believer is more likely to adapt to the challenges of the modern world and more able to contribute to the group's welfare.

I - Refusing to adapt and change, to broaden its tolerance, and to give up all beliefs in the supernatural will cause a mainstream religion to die. Religion based on delusions of the supernatural should be opposed by objective scientific evidence, and the best ethical and moral (in the right sense) standards.

4. Obesity and the Law, and How Not to be Fat

I attempted a blog post on this subject and failed miserably. It is a sensitive subject and I have no desire to make anyone feel bad. **(Note: I have since revised and posted my more controversial thoughts on this subject. This is actually my second try. It includes some things I have learned about fitness and nutrition. I am no scientist, but I have read more than a dozen of the popular books and have summarized them for you here. Hope it helps:**

In America, Race, Gender Preferences, Religion, and Obesity are confounding subjects. They provoke powerful emotions, generate hateful prejudices, and have maddeningly elusive solutions. I posted my views on organized religion in a note on my personal Facebook, since I believe such views are essentially personal, but obesity impacts legal issues from every angle.

West Virginia, in spite of our rugged hills, pioneer heritage, and avid devotion to sports, leads the nation in obesity, with all the resultant problems that fact implies.

In divorce, obesity effects intimacy, the health of the parents, self-image and health of the children, and in employment and insurance.

In personal injury, juries are very "judgmental" of obese claimants. Fat people usually have more serious pre-existing conditions. They are more susceptible to injury, and a fit person is much more likely to come out of a collision unscathed than his overweight counterpart.

I can turn a pre-existing injury into an advantage in a personal injury claim. I have explained that in other blog posts. A person with a bad back or knee, quite simply, is more susceptible to injury than one who does not have a weak back or knee, but making that argument is hard for a fat person, even when over half of the jury is probably significantly overweight.

I tend not to gain a lot of weight. That is a blessing. I was around 150 lb. in college and have made it as high as 180. But, that extra 15-20 lb. (I sit here today almost exactly between those two numbers), is what keeps the blood levels out of whack, appearance less than optimal, and fitness far from ideal.

When I encounter a problem: how to race a car, maintain a pond, play an instrument, run an office, or lose some weight, I tend to read a book on the subject. (Am still looking for that book to tell me how to maintain our one acre farm pond!)

That's why I have read 15-20 books over the years on nutrition, weight-loss, and fitness.

Here is a summary of what I know:

A. **Fast reps and vigorous activity increases endurance and cardio-vascular health;**

B. **Slow reps and heavier weights increase bulk and strength.** But, there are many gradations between these concepts.

C. **People who cut way back on calories lose weight. But....;**

D. **Most of us cannot cut way back on calories for very long,** especially if their diet is low fat (Dean Ornish, Weightwatchers, Jenny Craig, etc.). Note: since writing this, I read an interesting article in Wired Magazine which reports that "Weightwatchers" has been completely revamped to a much closer approximation of a "Mediterranean" or "low carb" nutrition plan. The core of Weightwatchers is the network of support, the structure, and the social component. Not a bad idea for lots of people.

E. **My favorite is the Mediterranean diet; lean meat, plenty of veggies, olive oil, some butter, whole wheat bread, seafood, beans, etc.**

F. Some people cannot lose weight on this diet, so they are told to starve themselves.

G. **Some people cannot gain weight** and even have digestive or colon issues that make it very difficult to maintain proper body weight.

H. **They have tested some very unhappy laboratory rats on starvation diets, and some human beings even ascribe to these diets,** and they may live an extra 10% to 20% (Those who do not put a bullet through their heads; the people, not the rats, who must simply endure.)

I. **The book I read recently, "Why We Get Fat; And What to Do About It" by Gary Taubes, and "The Atkins Diet Revolution" and many magazine and Internet news articles, make one compelling point, over, and over, in many inexorable compelling and logical ways.**

J. **That point is that for 99.9999% of mankind's (humankind's) existence, there was NO OBESITY PROBLEM.** People did not get fat and could not get fat.

K. **Apparently, we were always omnivorous,** but we ate few grains, no potatoes, and everything else "rough." We ate the entire animal, insect protein, the fish we could catch, and anything that moved, wriggled, or grew naturally.

L. **Some diets now promote this "paleo" diet.** (I have since downloaded "The Paleo Diet" to kindle. I have no quarrel with it but believe there are some less drastic, more scientifically based, alternatives.

M. **Since the Chinese, Koreans, Japanese, and other cultures, at least until they began to take on our eating habits, have not had serious obesity problems, the paleo diet is not the only way we can survive today.**

N. **Scientific studies and testing agree that Americans are fat because of SUGAR,** aka, carbohydrates, aka, "carbs."

O. **Carbs are table sugar, high fructose sugar, honey, cornstarch, but also, wheat, rice, potatoes, and therefore noodles, pasta.** Carbs are also sweet corn, cookies, cake, bagels, sweetened yogurt, bread, Ding Dongs, Twinkies, ice cream cones, crackers, and even beans, yellow veggies, and nuts.

P. **Low "net carbs" are good?** That's because they are mixed with something called "fiber." It is GOOD that we have to work hard to sort out the fiber from the sugar. It must take our bodies a lot of effort. I am shocked to know my Atkins breakfast bars have actual sugar. Why not NutraSweet??!! They taste like chocolaty sweet crap, but one each morning is only 2-4 "net carbs."

Q. **Sometime between when I was a kid and now, "they" invented the food pyramid.** "They" knew that carbs are the very cheapest food, that we love the taste (think potato chips, fries, and all the stuff in Para. 16 above.), and "they" knew that food with fat in it just had to be bad for you.

R.   **"They" just knew that exercise will help you lose weight. Only trouble is, IT WON'T!!!"** Remember when Bill Clinton jogged to McDonalds?

S.   **Exercise and good nutrition are good for you,** but exercise is much better for keeping your bones healthy, muscles toned and strong, and heart and circulatory system healthy, than for losing weight.

T.   **"They" forgot that working out makes you "hungry as hell."**

U.   **They decided to say things like "a potato is full of nutrients,** especially if eaten with no butter or salt." How many of us want to eat a potato without butter, margarine, or gravy?? Or sour cream, or honey......... or?

V.   **Potatoes turn into pure sugar, even without piling on the "good stuff."**

W.   **If you read "Food Nation" or some other books on the subject, you will learn we eat many more magnitudes of sugar than the people in colonial times.**

X.   **More surprising is that a diet of few, if any, carbs, and plenty of proteins and fat, is quite healthful.**

Y.   **Once we remove the carbs, the body HAS TO burn off our stored fat.**

Z.   **This is the induction phase of Adkins.**

AA.   This part of Adkins was so controversial, that "The New Adkins Diet Revolution" stressed "the induction" phase as a temporary, 60-90-day stage.

BB.   Gary Taubes has **the nerve to say it is a perfectly <u>healthful</u>** (NOT HEALTHY!! We are healthy; food is, or is not, healthful.) nutritional regimen.

CC.   **So, this is what I concluded:**

    i.   **If you eat anything you want, test your blood and find it is optimum, then eat anything.**

    ii.   **If you like starving yourself, or eating incredibly low fat, and that keeps you at your ideal weight, feel free to do that, but don't keep firearms at your house. The stats are clear.**

    iii.   **If, as do most people, you can eat a reasonable amount of meat, fresh fruit (not juice), veggies, beans, whole wheat, nuts, cheese, and great stuff, and lose weight, AND CAN AFFORD THE GREATER COST, then that's the route to follow.**

    iv.   **But, if you just cannot lose any other way, consider the concept of proteins and fats and little, if any, carbs, and ignore the "tsk-tsk" of the "we hate fat and love carbs" people. Just be sure to have the right doctor and to monitor your health and blood levels.**

v.   **Whether it helps you lose weight or not!**

So,

A.   **Exercise your body; and,**

B.   **Exercise your mind, read, think, write, talk, even argue; do cross-word puzzles, and drag yourself away from the TV.**

At least, that's the way I see it.

5.   Burt's History of the World

This is the first part of a "history lesson" I wrote for our grandchildren, Anna, Jack, Grady, Lucille, Frances, and Finley. I include it in my blog because:

A.   It's what I am thinking about right now, and I write about what I am thinking about.

B.   If you are an intelligent person, you probably want to know if your potential lawyer (or your adversary) is intelligent. This will give you a hint.

C.   Maybe you will get an overview of history that will prompt you to read further, or maybe it will be the only history you read this month.

D.   I am also writing for myself a summation of the impressions I retain from a lifetime of reading, and the last ten years or so, especially including The Teaching Company's History of Ancient Egypt, a course on CD by Long Island University Professor Bob Briar

234

http://www.liu.edu/CWPost/Academics/Research/
Scholars/Bob-Brier . I commend it highly.

On my "reading to do list" are histories of China, India, Japan, and Korea. I will start with A History of East Asia by Charles Holcomb which I just downloaded to my Kindle. And, as I drove to work today, I heard of a new biography of Ben Franklin by Jonathan Lyons, The Society For Useful Things, the premise of which is the author's view of how Franklin led the movement to bring the Age of Enlightenment to American. It is that "Age" that launched mankind into the modern world.

My focus here is the middle of the Eurasian land mass, Egypt, Greece, Italy (Roman Empire), Greater Europe, and Byzantium. Why are they important, and why is so much of conflict of the world focused on this interface of the continents of Europe, Asia, and Africa? Interface? Perhaps part of the answer is in the question.

Here, kids, as CNN's best commentator Fareed Zakaria says, "is my take":

A.   Hominids diverged from the great apes and evolved in Southern Africa over 6 plus millions of years and migrated north through what is now the Middle East to Europe and Asia. How, why, and which species evolved? Start reading something by Richard Leakey, or Donald Johanson's, and Blake Edgar's "From Lucy to Language," Simon and Schuster, and others. It is a complex and fascinating story.

B.   If you have decent retention, you will have an idea of how mankind changed since we split from the great apes, and how we got where we are now.

C.   For 1.5 million years or so, there was one tool, a hand axe. Someone, an early Leonardo da Vinci, figured out that if you broke off a piece from flint, or chert, it creates a very sharp edge. Chert is a fine-grained silica-rich microcrystalline, cryptocrystalline or microfibrous sedimentary rock. Later, I figure, they also realized that it helps to have one that was pointed, leading to all sorts of things in a very slow blink of the eye.

D.   Near Egypt, to the West, and elsewhere, there developed smaller knives, drills, scrapers, projectile points, and atl atl's (sticks with a groove, to lengthen the arm and fling the projectile farther than man can do with his arm alone); slings, and bows and arrows. We were on our way toward nuclear weapons and iPads. Professor Brier gives a good summary of how things developed for the 700,000 years before the Egyptian upper and lower kingdoms united.

E.   As for the Geography; just look at this: Start on the large map below, at just above Spain and travel due East 8000 miles or so. Land, land, land, wide and deep. According to Author Jared Diamond, having so much land at the same latitudes meant that many more diverse species, and germs, and organisms, can develop than on continents like North and South America and Australia.

F.   Then check out the Americas. They are tall, tall, tall and narrow, and have barriers to communication such as water, deserts, swamps, and mountains. Also, with changes in latitude effecting the climate, species have less opportunity to diversify. And be sure to notice that the west coast of Europe and Africa match up nicely with the East Coast of the Americas and remember that once they were part of one huge continent called Gondwanaland. It's another piece of a gigantic puzzle. Many species can be tracked back to the time the continents separated.

G.   From the Gulf of Mexico to the "S" in South America, the landmass is very narrow. But East to West in Eurasia, has lots of landmass with similar climates; so, the variety of species, animal and plants, was much greater, and the number of plants and animals that were domesticated was much larger. Just look at a world map and you will see.

H.   As animals were domesticated, living with man, their germs and diseases easily spread. With so much space at one latitude, diversity existed, and with so much animal/man contact, disease spread, and immunities developed.

I.   Thus developed the ability of European explorers and settlers to wipe out Native Americans with their germs. But let's get back to the area in question.

J.   Australia is pretty big, and there are all those Islands to the East and north, but Australia is mostly desert, again with narrow bands of habitable land. Its separation from the other continents led to the evolution of different species into nooks occupied by other creatures in the other continents. Mankind arrived there relatively late, homo sapiens, sapiens, modern man.

K.   So, what an amazing stew existed in the lands surrounding the Mediterranean Sea 10,000 years ago.

L. Food producing plants and grasses were gathered, concentrated, and eventually planted and harvested. Agriculture developed, and the leaders of the Upper Nile (to the South!), and the Lower Nile (to the North) (Remember, the Nile runs from South to North), distinguished by the shape (tall and short) and color (white and red) of their headdresses, somehow united. There was a tremendous burst of civilization, creativity, myth-making, writing, and technical advance.

M. Mankind knew so little, that some with imagination, and, I suspect, a desire to lead and control, claimed special knowledge and insights. Some stumbled onto hallucinogens. Others fasted and followed paths such as asceticism. They saw visions, had dreams, and began what appears to be a universal trait of mankind, to find answers, even without evidence to support them. Jean Auel writes wonderful reconstructions of our world @ 40,000 years ago in The Clan of The Cave Bear series. Her protagonist Ayla invents nearly everything, including modern medicine. I think her description of the ancient wizard or medicine man, or shaman, rings true. Reference The Shamans of Prehistory by Jean Clottes and David Lewis-Williams, Harry N. Abrams, Inc.

N. And, myth and invention co-existed with fact. (Strangely, in many places, including much of America, it still does.) A priest who could predict the likely return of the flooding of the Nile, or frost, or a migrating food source, would be mighty valuable, regardless of what he believed caused it. And the ability to predict the time and place of the return of a comet, or eclipse seemed magical.

O.   From the beginning, was the tug and pull of the religious and the secular(political).

P.   Priests had special knowledge, such as anticipated dates of the recurrent flooding. The world was a scary place, storms, extreme cold, heat, and drought, earthquakes, volcanoes, and, of course, floods. The legend of the great flood predates, by a thousand years, the story of Noah, notwithstanding the claims of Old Testament, and the worst movie of all time, Noah.

Q.   But, perhaps first between the "alpha males" of the extended family, then the tribe, regional groups, countries, and alliances, political power and organization allowed groups to compete and succeed.

R.   Back to Egypt, in a relatively short time, during "The Old Kingdom," the shape of the pyramids was perfected. Then the great age of pyramid building ended, but not the construction of tombs, coffins, temples, obelisks, and statues. Egypt survived because it refused to change, and the flooding of the Nile was so predictable, and the neighbors were so "conquerable" for ages and ages. Pharaohs did well when they were young and vigorous enough to go into battle themselves in order to vanquish their enemies. Egypt tended to falter when their Pharaoh survived to old age, or failed to have a competent male heir.

S.   Professor Brier does a brilliant job of tying it all together, showing the flow, the stability, subtle change, and details such as mummies, diseases, myths, animals, hieroglyphics, and foods. Ancient Egypt finally ends with Cleopatra, and the death of her children.

T.   Then another huge burst, the classic period of Greece, the fact based "legend of Troy" Greek mythology, and philosophical thought, something that never occurred to the Egyptians, who were obsessed with the afterlife. Seneca, Socrates, Plato, and Aristotle to name a few names.

U.   Pathagoras, and, of course, Zeno and his famous paradox. In what seemed overnight, mankind was asking profound questions. Zeno pondered infinity with the question, "How can an arrow move and occupy a particular point in time."

V.   Then there was the development of the stage, and Greek tragedies and comedies, of which I know very little. The key was that an environment existed to foster thinking and philosophizing, among a relative few, just thousands, much as occurred later during The Reformation, Renaissance, and Age of Enlightenment, The Industrial Age, and The amazing Age of Information, later on.

W.   Greece predated Rome in its conquests, the Spartans and Athenians, the battles against Persia, the Peloponnesian War, Alexander the Great, and the powerful and persistent influence called Hellenism into which the Christian religion merged. The New Testament's St. Paul was a Hellenist. As I understand the Greek philosophers, and this I think is key, they perceived the world is essentially perfect, with ideal forms for what was the natural order of things. This jibed with Christian doctrine of the time. That perception would not change for nearly 2000 years.

X.   The successor of Greece was Rome. Predated by a mysterious people called The Etruscans, Rome lasted around 1000 years, less than one third of ancient Egypt.

Y.   The Romans adopted the Greek mythology, and renamed the Gods with Latin Names. While criticized for a lack of originality, they were great organizers, and centuries under foreign tyranny made Rome highly resistant to attempts to subdue them.

Z.   The Roman Republic became the Roman Empire, and its conquests, laws, civilization, and power spread throughout all areas surrounding the Mediterranean Sea.

AA.   The Punic wars, with Carthage (Hannibal and his elephants, etc.), finally ended with Rome in control of a huge portion of the civilized world. Contrary to Egypt, which marched out year after year, conquered, stole, and returned with booty and tribute, The Roman Empire conquered set up its towns, forts, baths, temples, and stadia in the conquered territories, and set up its occupants as Roman citizens. Barbarians and foreigners developed the traits of Rome. They became Roman.

BB.   Persistently and recurrently, aggressive peoples north of Italy, the Barbarians, attempted to defeat Italy.

CC.   Gibbon, in four huge volumes, "The Decline and Fall of the Roman Empire," which I have not yet conquered, blames corruption and Christianity for the eventual destruction of Rome.

DD.   In the 400's, the final Roman emperor, Romulus Augustus, passed from the scene.

EE.   The center of Christianity moved to Constantinople, site of modern Istanbul in Turkey. The great administrator Justinian gathered the laws throughout the realm and created a uniform system of law.

FF.   The struggle between Rome and Constantinople, Byzantium, especially as the center of Christendom, continued for 1100 years.

GG.   Efforts to revive Rome continued intermittently, but "the Dark Ages" persisted for another 1000 years or so.

HH.   The few learned persons, Christian monks, etc., looked back in wonder at the age and learning of Greece, Aristotle, and Plato.

II.   Science did not exist. It was a world of magic, fear, war, and ignorance, The Dark Ages.

JJ.   Pardon me for being unduly vague here, but the Dark Ages ended. The Italian Renaissance, Michelangelo, Galileo, Botticelli, a Revival of Rome, and growth of Florence, and Venice occurred. (I just summarized 2000 pages into a sentence!)

KK.   Venice was an island state that evolved as the inhabitants of Northern Italy periodically fled to outer islands for safety from the barbarians. (Another 1000 pages!) Finally, they got tired of being dislodged, so with some amazing building techniques, they constructed buildings and ships and stayed on their

242

island empire permanently. Venice turned to Byzantium and away from Rome. It still has cultural influences from the North and the West.

LL.   The Pope and Roman Catholic Church were so corrupt that Luther, with the help of German Barons and France's Frances I, commenced The Reformation, a revolution against the corruption of the Catholic Church.

MM.   Thanks to a gift from my wife Nancy, I have some idea of the conflict between Christianity and Islam. <u>Defenders of the Faith – Christianity and Islam Battle for the Soul of Europe</u>, by James Reston, Jr., Penguin Books.

NN.   Charles V of Spain became The Holy Roman Emperor thanks to the salacious salesmanship of the Pope, Clement VII. Reston describes him as "The woebegone Medici Pope Clement VII, powerless and self-pitying."

OO.   Charles V's great enemy in the mid-1500's is Suleyman the Magnificent. There were a number of epic battles and close calls, sieges, taking of forts, and sea battles, which ended with Islam not conquering Europe. It is hard to imagine it otherwise, but it was a pretty close call. Lucky the Moslems were not the administrators the Romans were.

PP.   Then there burst forth the most brilliant burst of intellectual and scientific energy in the history of the world. It is called "The Age of Enlightenment." I have mentioned it in other writing, and a client of mine did a very good book report mentioned in my post below.

The story of the British Royalty Society is the story of that era. Descartes, Newton, Spinoza, Leibniz, Locke, Galileo, Brahe somehow breaking out of the darkness, and virtually inventing the scientific method.

QQ.   Sir Isaac Newton, perhaps the most powerful mind of all time, also wrote a detailed, but useless analysis of the scriptures, and was a master alchemist. Galileo remained an avowed believer in God, as Darwin later claimed, even as they were disproving "him."

RR.   Here is my client's report which I published with his permission in Amazon. com, "The Clockwork Universe: Isaac Newton, the British Royal Society, and the Birth of the Modern World," by Edward Dolnick. http://wp.me/p4utce-3E.

SS.   Much of my recent reading is referenced in this blog post, "A Small Town Lawyer's Reading List," http://wp.me/p4utce-40; These are some of the books I have read in the last several years to lead me to conclusions I will cover in Part 2.

Lest we get too caught up with ourselves, I suggest you spend a couple minutes to view the perspective that Carl Sagan had on our "small blue dot": https://www.youtube.com/watch?v=p86BPM1GV8M .

6.   Burton Hunter's Criticism of Religion and Religiosity

WONDERS OF NATURE

I have noted with interest the passionate Facebook p
over politics and religion, and the invocation of supernat
powers to help us avoid, or recover from, disaster. I have even implored the great Spaghetti Monster for intervention. I believe in the power of prayer, people rooting for one another, encouraging each other, and seeking power from "somewhere." I think we all benefit by knowing we are not alone in this journey called life.

However, I agree with Elizabeth Edwards that we are naive to seek assistance from an intervening sentient God to cure our cancer, or as I prayed last night, to help me find the missing Buddy the Dog.

I WONDER WHAT'S GONE WRONG? NEWTOWN CONNECTICUT

I awoke this morning and immediately thought about yesterday's horrific shooting in Ct. My wife Nancy called her Mother Marjorie on Friday afternoon. She had been crying all day. Marjorie is 91 years old, and she lives about 20 minutes from the shooting scene. Around 9:40 a.m. she was driving to the store when the state trooper in front turned on his siren and lights and made a 180 turn and headed toward Sandy Hook and New Town.

Newtown is an idyllic New England town. We have driven through it dozens of times, when I was stationed at Griffiss A.F.B. in Rome, New York and when going to and from some of our favorite places, Lime Rock Park, Lakeville, Stockbridge Ma., and The Red Lion Inn. It is our portal to the Berkshire Mountains. There used to be a historic restaurant, The Yankee Drover. It burned, but it's flag staff may still be there.

scares here in Upshur County in recent
mily law lawyer, I have received my share
been associated with a number of fatalities.
two-week murder trial and had a client
nd murder. The sentence was twenty-two
out after @ 14 years and has returned to
farming. .   can occur anywhere.

Of course, there are myriad legal issues associated with something like yesterday. Criminal law, privacy, security regulations, education, mental hygiene, and gun control, are just a few of them.

People struggle to understand how someone could shoot to death twenty innocent children, and their teachers and counselors. The reaction is predictable:

A.   The shooter was "evil," sent by the "Devil;"

B.   It was "God's will."

C.   It is time for "gun control."

D.   The Scientologists may note the person was taking an anti-psychotic drug or anti-depressant and blame the drug itself. In their world there is no such thing as a brain illness, cognitive disorder, or "mental illness." They prescribe a form of religious "voodoo" for people diagnosed with such conditions.

E.   Religious people have great difficulty during these times. If they believe in a sentient God who is pulling the strings behind the scene, they fumble all over themselves to explain how God "allowed" the event to happen.

F. Two weeks ago our guest minister, retired and over 70, patiently explained that Hurricane Sandy was sent by God as a sign that Jesus' second coming is around the corner. Why God decided to cause billions of dollars in storm damage and kill hundreds of people to make his point is not clear. And what of the great tsunamis that kill thousands?

G. I refuse to give God credit for a child that was saved by a courageous teacher, because to do so would require me to blame "him" for killing the others. And, ascribing Hurricane Sandy to God means he kills people when he gets angry. That's pretty "Old Testament" and hardly in keeping with Jesus' teachings, in which the focus is on love and forgiveness.

H. The gun control advocates go on a rant almost immediately, without even pausing to show respect to the very real, flesh and blood, victims.

I. The NRA and gun ownership advocates go into a full court press reminding politicians of the tremendous political clout they yield. Imagine what they are planning at this very moment to protect their turf.

J. The press always asks, "What should parents tell their children?"

K. Everyone asks, "How could this happen?"

L. Sometimes the killer is a sociopath and "simply" vicious and angry. More often, it seems the person was "deranged." The news media cannot wrap their heads around "deranged." They just do not seem to try.

M. The most misunderstood illness seems to be schizophrenia. I have not heard the press, or the experts, explain that a person affected with this emperor of brain diseases may be terrified and hallucinating.

N. I spent considerable time with a young man in the secure psychiatric ward at Chestnut Ridge. The anti-psychotic drugs were not really reaching him. He explained that the F.B.I. had singled him and his family, for assassination Therefore, he was armed at all times. He knew that they were going to come to his door, knock, and kill him.

O. I asked him if he knew he was mentally ill, and he assured me that he did, and he knew that his brain was not processing information correctly, BUT he still tracked each person that walked by his house, confident when the real assassin showed up, he would know him and kill him. That was pretty scary.

P. This was a peaceful, intelligent, articulate, but very sick, young man, who did not want to hurt anyone except the assassin. He could shoot several people as they walked to his door and be considered a monster even though, in his mind, he was defending himself from a demon or alien who was trying to kill him.

Q. As I write this, I do not know if the Ct. shooter believed God had told him these children were evil and had to be killed, were actually aliens from outer space, or that God had decided to call them back home and he was the tool by which God's instructions were to be carried out. His actions may make perfect sense, if his thoughts were accurate.

So, what do I think?

A.   There is no evidence there is anyone "pulling the strings." I refer you to my article, "Burt's Views on Religion and Religiosity." http://tinyurl.com/6lu7dyx

B.   I wish my intelligent, but religious, friends, at times like these would remember and acknowledge that their comments about God's love and intervention are metaphors, and that supernatural events do not take place, and that certain terrible events are going to occur because of our nature as animals walking this earth. And storms and earthquakes are bound to happen because of the nature of our physical universe.

C.   Brains will malfunction, people will act out violently, and no super hero, demon, or God, is making these events occur.

D.   Regardless of my skepticism, I still pray for the victims and their family. Why? First, I believe that wishing someone well and asking "someone" to look out for them is a good thing. What harm can it do? I believe that sensing the pain of others, empathizing, and hoping for their recovery, helps the person who prays. While the subjects of the prayer probably cannot "feel" it, letting them know we are praying for them may help give them strength. It's a reminder to them they are not alone and that others care.

E.   Our society is dealing with accelerating rapid change. It is fragmenting. Here is an example. Nancy and I are news junkies, so after an event like yesterday, we may watch 5-10 hours of coverage per day. We tend to feel others must be doing the same thing, BUT THEY AREN'T!!!!!!!!:

i.   My staff of busy young mothers hardly even watch TV, and when they do, it is probably children's TV.

ii.   In Nov. 1963, we had nothing to watch but the aftermath of John F. Kennedy's death. As a result, I saw Jack Ruby shoot Lee Harvey Oswald.

iii. In 1956, when I was ten, and while visiting my Great Aunt Jenny Morris in Cambridge Ohio, the only TV programming, on any of the three channels, was the Democratic National Convention. Thus, since I could not fish every minute, and my elderly aunt and her husband were not inclined do anything with their young guest, except eat meals with him, I read and watched the convention. (Aunt Jenny's husband Frank was retired from the Railroad, so I got to ride the train by myself from Wheeling for free.)

iv.   The terrified, highly religious, "I don't want the modern world to ruin my life!" people focus on their family and church. They give up their education and critical thinking and limit their reading and their education to religious based material. They have assigned reading, prayer groups, the Sunday service, religious books, and choir. No time for studying and thinking for themselves.

v.   Many children are watching TV and the Internet without their parents, and viewing things that their parents never see.

vi.   As sick as the fellow in Newtown may have been, he still must have tapped into the creepy mass killing, gun culture, the Gothic, and anti-society culture of the Internet, and of high violence video games, the purchase and use of body armor, and hatred, plenty of hatred.

vii.   Non-mentally ill "haters" can easily locate neo-Nazi and other racists materials on line. They feed on the hatred and myths of the other haters.

viii.   Gay Americans can focus on "gay culture;" Blacks on "black culture;" and Hispanics, on Spanish language TV. Racing fans even have their racing channel, such as it is.

ix.   The porn watchers are in their golden age. They are sophisticated, and there are horrible networks that exchange and circulate child porn. Many of my divorce cases have "online sex" as a main causal factor.

x.   There are tens of thousands of people dedicated to using the Internet to cheat and steal by schemes and hacking. Wired Magazine advises that soon password protection will be passé.

xi.   Billions are being spent on international drug trafficking. It is a cancer upon our society.

xii. Terrorists are coordinating their plans to attack America and symbols of "Western Culture" worldwide.

xiii. No one has to worry about being stuck with only a nature documentary, 60 Minutes news program, or "serious" play or movie. With 200 channels, why bother? Just switch to something more "entertaining." That's what I would have done in 1956 if I could have.

xiv. A very small slice of the mass of viewers watches public TV and listens to public radio, orders college level course from The Learning Company, or accesses hundreds of thousands of free online college courses.

xv. There is online higher education, much which is apparently accredited and excellent, but people, being people, have borrowed billions in student loans but are unable to stay motivated long enough to get their degrees. How can we stay focused in such a fragmented world?

xvi. Our public and private schools are expected to provide much more than a good education. They must make up for parents who do not prepare nutritious foods, love to those who are abused and neglected, and provide child care and discipline to the undisciplined. The family can no longer be trusted to provide the moral and social framework.

xvii. Whatever they are learning, kids no longer seem to know WHERE things are located,

WHAT happened in our past, WHERE a comma or semi-colon goes, or HOW to spell. This lack of fundamental skills is obvious, even in the wonderful intelligent women who work for me. An employer must be ready to train and educate his work staff. That's not right.

xviii. Kids get to listen only to the music they and their friends want to listen to. Mom, Dad, Grandma, and Grandpa may listen to their oldies, to blues, jazz, and even the classics, but with buds in their children's ears, the parents only know their kids' music is intolerable, and the children know only what their peers know.

xix. "Good parents," even those who aren't hiding in their churches, still want to protect their children, so they may shield them from so much that the young adult is overwhelmed with temptation when they move to the freedom of college life.

xx. Other parents allow the kids to watch what they watch, hear what they hear, and fail to provide a steady commentary to children on their personal values. Maybe their values are wanting.

xxi. Institutions like Boy Scouts, Girls Scouts, and 4-H were a powerful compliment to school (curricular and extra-curricular) home, and church in the 50's and 60's.

xxii. Nowadays the children of my divorce clients often have no extra-curricular activity and no organizations. Two working parents may not be able to be an adult leader for volunteer.

The solution? I DO NOT KNOW!

A. If you cannot claim your "can't helps" were handed down from God, or that violators will not "burn in hell," how can you get people to conform to reasonable standards?

B. If the Internet is uncensored, and we are committed to freedom of thought and speech, and tolerance, how can we have common values?

C. I say focus on education and child rearing and nutrition/fitness.

D. We know that the American diet is killing us. Let's do a better job educating people on nutrition and control the child's diet and activity at school.

E. Let's transition our religion, before it largely disappears, so that an intelligent, educated, person is not turned off by the focus on the Jesus cult and the supernatural. Somehow, make room for the skeptic. If Jesus' teachings cannot stand on their own, without the threat of a burning hell or promise of everlasting life, what good is it to the living?

F. Let's establish a new set of accepted standards, civility, morality, sobriety, diminished violence, tolerance, honor, honesty (no stealing, lying or cheating!), cleanliness, and moderation. But let's not be too judgmental of those who fall short. Encourage them to try again.

G.   Let's regulate our children's TV and radio programming. Yes, Republicans,

        REGULATE! Let's make it fun, science based, informative, stimulating, and uplifting.

H.   Let's foster a new sense of discipline, moderation, and culture in our society. ("Old Fashioned Values" without old fashioned superstition and ignorance.)

I.   Let's raise a generation of moral scientists, engineers, and teachers, to cure cancer, move mankind into outer space, protect our planet, improve our health, and create the infrastructure of a mobile and literate society.

That should be a pretty good start. But first, let's pay our respects to those dead people, their families, and community.

7.   A Great Challenge for America: Violence

Where do we start? With our animal nature? Our tribal past? Our "Colt and Winchester" frontier myths? Our warlike natures? Our vicious propensity for war? Our distrust of anyone who is different? Our belief in myths as fact? The exploding "Age of Information"? Racial and gender-based hatred?

I will assume "all of the above" and proceed accordingly.

I think having a historical and anthropological perspective is essential to thinking of this challenge clearly. It can dispel the belief that we are somehow special, touched by God, with a pre-determined future. Realizing that we are "simply" an advanced ape-mammal is essential. If we insist we are different, special, created by God in his form, we keep looking for a supernatural "savior" when there is none. The only "salvation" is within us, what we are, and what we may become.

I also think that a view toward the future, a grounding in science and technology, and an appreciation of the remarkable explosion of progress we've had (starting with seeds before the Age of Enlightenment), and an appreciation of "accelerating change," are essential.

We know that people have been fantasizing and dreaming for over 30,000 years as evidenced by the French cave paintings and the pregnant fertility doll from Germany. What a coincidence that those are the things that interest me. One of our best dreams can be a safe America, with the lowest gun violence in the world.

MY PERSPECTIVE

I have a "liberal education," a good science and math foundation from high school, a misapplication of my energy in college but still lots of reading, three years of learning the structure and philosophy of the law, and 46 years of representing individuals in all manner of conflict. I have supplemented my adult personal and professional experiences with reading that tends to be heavy on "information," including science for the educated lay reader.

I grew up next to a farm, worked there for six summers, had a bolt action .22 rifle, five years of military prep school, and "marksmanship" training, and four years as a USAF JAG. I am not against private gun ownership. I am a lifetime Republican who is done with the Republican Party. I am a generalist!

But, think of the specialists, the people who understand the inner workings of the atom, the scientists who have cracked the secret of the genome, the brilliant economists and "big data" psychologists who are analyzing the behavior of millions of people and billions of transactions, and the mathematicians and physicists who understand "relativity," black holes, the expanding universe, and "The Big Bang" that created our world.

I am glad to know that such puzzles exist but am not bright or specialized enough to figure it all out.

There are a tiny few "polymaths" who somehow seem to have synthesized a great deal of it. I guess I might aspire to be a "mini-poly," just smart enough to get a glimpse into the infinite and to articulate some practical suggestions. As meager as my accomplishments are, I am sad that a large portion of our citizens are swimming and breathing in waters they do not even know exist. They won't read this or agree if they do.

I strongly encourage anyone who aspires to an understanding of our most puzzling country to read Fantasyland: How America Went Haywire: a 500 Year History by Kurt Andersen.

https://tinyurl.com/y98wtddf

It gave me insights that reading a dozen books on related topics the last few years has not. The short summary is that this country of immigrants has its own peculiar ability to have dreams, goals, and myths that are not grounded in fact. We "baby boomers" include a disturbing percentage of members who somehow have grown into adulthood believing we can stay "young at heart," or childlike, our whole lives. Many of us dress like kids and gorge on porn, video games, and fantasy (e.g. sports leagues) and "holy roller" churches. A startling number of people, devout and not devout, believe in a God that interacts and monitors people, punishes them, rewards them, and acts out in petulance. And there are thousands, no millions, who pander to these beliefs and profit from them. These beliefs are false and destructive to our adaptation to the modern world.

I have written that without addressing the question, "How do we reduce gun violence in America?" It is a subject akin to arguing about religion. The more we argue, it seems the more entrenched we become. Here are my thoughts:

THE NATURE OF GUN VIOLENCE

Gun violence is a symptom like fever, pain, or that itching rash. We of course want to alleviate symptoms, but that will not cure the underlying disease. We must address the disease and the side effects of any treatment. While treating to control the sneeze and wheeze, we still want to solve the riddle of cancer and heart disease. Violence, oppression, greed, and hatred are the diseases. Bump stocks and semi-automatic rifles are the symptoms.

If you want a peek at the foundation upon which these comments stand, here are a few ideas, articles I have written, on related subjects and suggested sources:

http://hunterlawfirm.net/burts-history-of-the-world-part-i-to-the-age-of-enlightenment/

http://hunterlawfirm.net/a-small-town-lawyers-reading-list/

http://hunterlawfirm.net/burts-criticism-of-religion-and-religiosity/

http://hunterlawfirm.net/symantics-metaphor-religion-and-clarity-of-thought/

http://hunterlawfirm.net/the-challenge-to-the-church-in-the-modern-world-or-whats-it-all-about-anyhow/

http://hunterlawfirm.net/the-formative-effect-on-a-country-boy-of-the-4-h-clubs-in-ohio-county-wv-in-the-50s-and-60s/

http://hunterlawfirm.net/a-modern-view-of-religion-by-a-spiritual-person/

http://hunterlawfirm.net/burts-response-to-the-challenges-of-the-modern-world/

http://hunterlawfirm.net/i-wonder-whats-gone-wrong-newtown-connecticut/

WHY GUN VIOLENCE IS THE SYMPTOM

Mass killings seem to feed off "The Information Age." They follow a pattern as if the perpetrators have read the same "How To" manual. In a way they have. Each tragedy plays out the same on the news. What happened? How many dead? Who were the heroes? Who was the perpetrator? Why did no one stop him? Were there warning signs? Who were the victims? What were their stories? Who are the scapegoats? Who can we blame it on? How quickly can one side of the gun violence issue accuse the other one of politicizing it?

I can hear regret in the reporters' voices as they inevitably help to make the shooter famous. And, somewhere, another warped and broken person is thinking, "Wow, look at how important that shooter is. I can do that."

So, gun violence is a symptom of our troubled age and our difficulties in adjusting to accelerating change. 150 years ago, a death was tragic, but everyone in America did not get to share it in real time.

And, vicious ideas could and did spread, but at the speed of a horse or boat or train. Now it is the speed of light.

In the Wikipedia Age, the experts are hard to spot. Twenty years ago, we could trust The Encyclopedia Britannica to find the best scholars in their field and put one curated version on the page. Libraries were organized by The Dewey Decimal System.

Now, people compete to fit the truth into Wikipedia. Much seems to be accurate, but it is a different world. As divorce rates skyrocket, marriage rates drop, parents lose the ability to be gatekeepers of their children's information, and the problems grow. So, a key to my proposed solutions is a "Manhattan Project" or "Man on the Moon" effort to teach our people, adults and children, how to curate and evaluate the flood of "The Information Age." If we fail, America, even if it survives, is facing chaos.

WHAT KINDS OF LAW?

We've heard it all. "It's not the gun; it's the person holding the gun." "It's a mental health issue." "The only way to deal with a bad guy with a gun is a good guy with a gun." "They want to take our guns." "Secure the schools." "Harden the targets." The problem is the men; get rid of men." Really?

From the NRA is mostly silence. They don't even make the argument that I would make for them. They have abandoned their original purpose, to support the sportsman, the hunters and hobbyists, to promote gun safety, and to train gun users in the safe and responsible use of these inherently dangerous tools, tools designed expressly to kill and maim.

Gun manufacturers and The NRA are willing to say or do anything to keep gun sales going. Their reason to exist is selling guns.

Do we restrict gun sales? Register every gun? Limit magazine sizes? Restrict military style semi-automatic weapons? The type of ammunition? Require mental health screening? Limit "conceal and carry"? Place age limits on the purchase of firearms? Some of these subjects are toxic, but I say, "Let's consider everything and attack from many sides." This giant problem needs a multifaceted solution, not piecemeal Band-Aids.

Here are some ideas:

A. Personally, I think NPR is nuts to be interviewing someone about repealing the 2nd amendment. Perhaps the idea is to scare people into voting for regulations. My long article is almost done, but it is clear to me that we need to train those who wish to own a gun with the kinds of precision and ethical framework, be it hunting, self-protection, or sports, that reflects the dangerousness of the instrumentality. I'd say at least twice what driving a car requires. Compare The Skip Barber Racing School to your high school driving instructor.

B. I would have limits by age. I would have strict rules, age and qualifications, surrounding concealed and open carry. I would consider what to do about volunteer security personnel in schools but require at least the training in shooting that a state trooper gets.

C.   Yes to <u>universal</u> background checks. All weapons, even my Grandpa's 100 plus year old single shot .22. Should be registered. No special privileges for gun shows. Big penalties for illegal weapon sales. Liability to gun manufacturers for people illegally killed with their inherently dangerous product. Once registered, I would have a computer chip in every gun. I would track every transfer. Punishment would not be big for people with clean records; say relinquishment of the gun, a fine or short jail sentence, or community service. Prison reform. Revision of our drug laws. Complete review of our mental and cognitive illness medical system.

D.   Outlaw gerrymandering and pass comprehensive campaign reform? Outlaw military style weapons unless a person meets very strict criteria.

E.   Bump stocks? Of course; even the president likes that one. That would be a start.

HOW DOES THIS RELATE TO ACCELERATING CHANGE?

By now you should have seen it. The line graph, low on the left, rising to the right, and zooming nearly vertical on the right side. This line chart mimics "accelerating change" towards what one authority calls "The Singularity." "The Singularity is Near: When Humans Transcend Biology," Ray Kurzweil, 2006.

I recently read a book called "Fantasyland – How America Went Haywire: A 500 Year History." I commend it to everyone. It reminds us that we once used words like "hokum," "malarkey," "con man," "scam," "balderdash," "hogwash," "confidence game," "poppycock," and "Buncombe," words used to reject a flamboyant but bygone era and welcome the modern world to America. The evidence is that we are falling back into a new "dark age." I hope I am wrong. The evidence says that the purveyors of myth, fantasy, and falsehood have a powerful new weapon that we have not learned to deal with. It began with TV but morphed and metastasized with the Internet.

Fantasyland also began because America went through at least a couple hundred years of idiocy, dreams of streets paved in gold, "end of the world," magic elixirs, medicine shows, carnivals, Mesmerism, Phrenology, homeopathic medicine, Mormonism, Scientology, conspiracy theories, and so much more. It is a multilayered book, but it reminds us that since the '60's, in America, people can pretty much believe anything they want, that the earth formed 4000 years ago, that people can rise from the dead, that flying saucers exist, that Princess Diana both planned her own death and died of a murder conspiracy, or that Elvis was just seen, alive and well, or a man can live in the belly of a whale for two days.

Donald Trump is the epitome of the "huckster," the "Carney," the "over-promiser," the liar, or as Fareed Zakaria properly quoted of him, "The Bullshit Artist."

But, how does an angry, maladjusted, mentally ill, evil, or "misled" individual come to believe that killing a bunch of people, mostly strangers, will solve anything? Those are complex questions. But, first I think we must focus on how to stop them.

INFORMATION OVERLOAD

I delete 50 extraneous e-mails each morning. I ignore the clamor of half a dozen news feeds. I decline a dozen books a day but still order three times what I can read. While I drive, I listen to audiobooks, podcasts, and Sirius XM. I still take a few magazines, Wired, Archeology Today, Road and Track, Car and Driver, and professional magazines. I send the e-mail I find useful to Evernote and the task list Wunderlist for future review and read the ones I "can't help" finding interesting. I scan paper documents, tag or archive, and hope I can find them when I need them. I try more than most, but information overload is real.

LOSS OF ETHICAL AND MORAL COMPASS

When our top political and religious leaders have learned that lying is better than telling the truth, to accomplish their venal goals, America is in trouble. Rush Limbaugh got it started when Congress repealed "the fairness doctrine" and "opinion news" entertainment was permitted.

http://www.pbs.org/wnet/tavissmiley/uncategorized/are-we-better-off-without-the-fairness-doctrine/

When our U.S. President is the best liar in the country, willing to say simply anything, and to contradict himself constantly, and we can't find a proper balance or bar to that, we are in trouble.

THE PROBLEM OF RELIGION

I was raised to believe that the truth is important and that lying, and liars, are bad. Now lying is not such a big deal. Americans, perhaps 25% of us, have reverted to a perverse, medieval, form of religion. The more fundamental for these groups the better. Each must have a supernatural leader, God, Savior, Prophet, Dictator, or Supreme Leader. Each totem performed supernatural miracles. Each claims a divine source for his teachings. The war of knowledge was fought, and science and rationality won, we thought?

But new evangelical and Pentecostal views and "new age relativity" and their teachers have returned to feed into the myth of the American Frontier, our rural heritage, our Southern supremacy, and our freedom to believe anything regardless of its factual basis. It is a backlash to progress, but it is real. Sorry, no room to explain this, but part of it grew out of the mythical "lost cause" of the post-Civil War South. Yesterday the pastor who led the prayer at the NASCAR race spoke to "The Lord" as if he were a favorite uncle asking him to return America to be "a Christian Nation" with every single citizen saved, and presumably, reborn in "the blood of Jesus Christ." Yuck. Before 1960, hardly anyone was "reborn." That's pretty much the end of me and NASCAR. Maybe I'm just hearing "same 'ol" for the first time, but it made me mildly ill. It is a sports event, NOT church!

THE PROBLEM OF SCIENCE

Science is a system for seeking objective truth. It requires experimentation, control of variables, patience, and a rigorous refusal to follow "wishful thinking." It is rational and empirical. It is technically amoral, but to me must be just as rigorously ethical.

But, Nazi's and even people in America came up with theories of dealing with racial minorities, inferiors, and defectives. Detractors of science decry objectivity, empirical thinking, and the rejection of intuition. They insist that if they FEEL strongly enough about something, we should concede its validity.

People who believe in "Natural Law" reasonably ask, "Where is the concept of right and wrong in science?" I struggle with that question, and I have accepted what former Supreme Court Justice Oliver Wendell Holmes, Jr. called "can't helps." These are core values of empathy, honesty, non-violence, compassion, equity, and fairness that my upbringing tells me are good for most people, in the sense that they can flourish and survive better if these values become the norm. I may be wrong but "can't help" feeling I am on to something.

PRISON REFORM

The history of crime and punishment in England holds many lessons. Credit Dickens with casting light on the plight of the poorest classes, a failed criminal system, and the "bleakness" of pollution filled cities. More recently, wholesale incarceration escalated in America during the Clinton era. It was well-intentioned, designed to deal with the drug crisis. But, with the highest percentage of incarcerations in the world, and 25 times (2500% of) the gun violence per capita in America than in other developed countries, we have created a crime manufacturing industry. In theory, we control these prisoners. In practice, we do not. Do we make sure they read Aristotle, Spinoza, Edward O. Wilson, Einstein, Darwin, Shakespeare, Martin Luther King, or Gandhi? Do we make sure they learn to read, write effectively, to calculate, to think critically, and to have a moral compass, to care for others? We do not! We allow them to collect into racial groups and cliques, to operate as gangs behind bars, use television as a drug, and allow them to organize for future criminal activity. Any dramatic decrease in gun violence will require a massive effort to reform our prisons.

DRUG REFORM

Our society teaches we must have more, we must have fun, we must be stimulated, we must be entertained, we must feel happy, and we must CONSUME. We are, after all, FANTASYLAND, where all views have equal weight, where criticism of anyone's faith is "fightin' words," and where getting high is no longer wrong.

MEDICAL REFORM

Our medical treatment system is broken. The power of drug companies, insurance companies, the corruption of our political system conspire so that it costs too much and does too little. Add to that a food industry that puts processed foods into our children, at school and at home, and the fact our diseases, to a large extent, are self-inflicted. That may not obviously connect to gun violence but obesity, lack of universal health care, and exorbitant costs constitute a huge challenge to America's social and medical health.

HEALING RACIAL DIVISIONS

"Fantasyland" helped me to understand the phenomena of police violence, racial conflict, the burning resentment of white working-class America, and the "southern mentality" Confederate Flags and the myth of the noble south.

OUR PROBLEMS WITH SEX AND GENDER

The success of birth control, break-down of morals, the progress the gay and transgender community have made, gay marriage, and the rest, have caused America to go bonkers over sex. That leads to anger and conflict and creates one more impediment toward solving our problems, including gun violence

GOD GAVE US A TOOL WE CANNOT HANDLE, OR EVEN FATHOM

The power of instant communication and computers in our hand beyond anything we imagined even twenty years ago have created a problem we are only now beginning to appreciate. It will take some of our best thinking to figure out now we can turn that tool away from porn and games and gambling to something positive.

TRAINING OUR YOUTH

We are not training our youth with the tools of our time. Smart devices, computers, and everything related to that is powerful. No one should be handling them without training, especially with the ethical foundation that makes their use positive and acceptable. We don't let 12-year-olds drive, and we don't let 15-year olds drive without an adult, and 16 years olds without a license.

THE ROLE OF REGULATION IN AMERICA

The evil nature of government regulations and rules is a myth. An orderly society must protect the young, the weak, the vulnerable, the poor, and promote an upward path for those who can achieve it while not letting wealth and power accumulate into the hands of a tiny few.

Our government must be powerful enough to control organized crime, terrorists, and the politically corrupt.

A young person should be learning core values and ethics from the playpen on. If parents aren't doing it, we must train the parents and the children.

Cars aren't designed to kill, but they can kill, and we regulate them. We regulate roads. We regulate industries, chemicals, zoning, sewage removal, water systems, housing, and drug production and sales. Look what happens when the regulation fails. You get the opioid and heroin crises!

The 2nd Amendment was an afterthought, part of the bill of rights, something that almost didn't make it into the US. Constitution. It is ambiguous, and it implies the right to bear arms is so we can form militias if we are threatened from the outside.

I concede that hunting, properly regulated, needs to remain in America. For sport? Food? Competition? Recreation? It is legal. And our society is not ready to say goodbye to it. Killing for trophies? Disgusting. Diminishing species to extinction? A profound crime.

MENTAL HEALTH

There are two devastating developments in medical treatment in my lifetime. The Opioid crisis, of course, was created by the push of the drugs industry to be unfettered in its prescription of addictive, powerful, pain medications FOR PROFIT. The other was the closing of our mental hospitals and the belief that the severely mentally ill could simply be turned loose and maintained by outpatient treatment.

I recently learned that "One Flew Over the Cuckoo's Nest," directed by Milos Foreman, written by Ken Kesey, and starring Jack Nicholson, was part of a major campaign to reject the concept of mental illness and promote the idea that any belief, strongly held, had some validity. The result of that revolution, during the Kennedy years, was an avalanche of homeless people and lost humanity.

If a doctor notices his patient is no longer capable of driving safely, it is his/her obligation to notify the Department of Motor Vehicles. If a psychiatrist or psychologist notices his patient lacks stability to operate a firearm safely, he should take similar action. How do they do that and maintain proper rapport and respect confidentiality with their patient? I am not sure, but some people who are mentally ill are dangerous, to themselves and sometimes to others.

SUMMARY

I believe we can require extensive training to operate such dangerous tools. I think fitness matters, sight matters, training matters, a stable mentality matters. Yes, I think each person should pass a mental and physical examination before getting a license.

I think we should monitor the Internet and use big data to spot the whackos.

I think we should train everyone in Internet ethics and etiquette.

I don't think young males should spend endless hours on games and porn; how to deal with that. I don't know. But they are subject to adult discipline and rules. Somehow, there need to be "rewards" for pursuing a positive and constructive course on the Internet. And, heaven forbid, censorship of child porn, porn, age appropriate, violence, racism, and hate speech, may not be the worst thing.

I think every parent should be certified in Internet safety and trained in how to protect their children. No certificate of completion, and our kids can't have a cell phone at school.

RELIGION

America believes everyone is entitled to believe whatever they want. Bullshit! That's a shame. If you believe that Jesus could fly without an airplane or Mohamed talked to God, or bushes burned without being consumed, you should be declared crazy and locked up. It is crazy. it is nuts. It is not true.

If you think that Buddha got it right in how to meditate, sacrifice and show empathy for the poor, great. If you think Jesus' teachings of poverty, charity, non-violence, compassion, tolerance, and the rest, are superior, fine. If you think black people and white people shouldn't hang out together, that's your view, but we probably should keep working on core ideas, honesty, compassion, sharing, cleanliness, conservation, responsibility to other life forms, preservation of our environment, tolerance and respect for others, WITHOUT claiming it comes from a supernatural honcho that only you and your little group are tuned into.

8.   *Fantasyland,* by Kurt Anderson

I have not been hit harder by a book in my life. Can't remember one that brought a more emotional response from my intelligent, loving, empathetic wife who listened to the last seven of twenty-four hours.

As a lifetime reader of science fiction, fiction, history, biography, and science, I wondered if anyone existed who believe as I do. Since I was a toddler being told of Santa, and realizing by age six that he didn't exist, I have been puzzling over the rational and irrational.

In Kurt Anderson, I find someone who mirrors, presents a foundation for, and explains, the world as I see it but could not fully explain.

How can a nation founded by men of the Age of Enlightenment be acting so utterly crazy? Anderson provides the foundation, wide and deep, carefully referenced, and writing extensively in the actual words of the purveyors of the fantasy of Fantasyland.

But, as he arrives at the 60's, the Hippies, Esalen Institute, talking in tongues, the rise of the religious right, false repressed memories, aliens, regression into past lives, The Satanist Cult murders, alien abductions, and "entertainers" becoming our leaders and sages, I began to get ill.

I agree that we can place the year 2000 as the point that our country became "fully fantasized," or, as Carl Sagan called it, "A Demon Haunted World." We have felt our founders got it right and we were on the way to a rational world. Wrong. We have been "rational" a very few years of mankind's myth-filled existence, and science and rational people are in for one hell of a fight. The outcome is very much in doubt. We may not be here for much longer.

For our children, our grandchildren, our country, and our world, we are very, very committed to this fight. I loved this book, every word.

This frees me from blaming God for trashing Japan or allowing little girls to be kidnapped, molested, and murdered. I found 3 things lately that helped affirm what I had figured out a long time ago:

A.   This morning there was a "coffee break" on NPR, an interview of two Muslim women, one rather devout, and one quite modern, on the eve of Ramadan. The devout one was pleased they were showing live feeds from Mecca, where unbelievers are banned from the entire city. The modern woman pointed out that there is a large superhighway into Mecca, but just outside the city, there is an off-ramp that says "non-believers exit here." She said Islam as practiced in Saudi Arabia is an abomination of the teachings of Mohamed and the worst interpretation in the world, especially in its treatment of woman. She pointed out that the Saudi version of Islam allows the beating of a woman for driving or having a wisp of hair showing from under her head covering. Converts who backslide, of course, are to be killed. She said that the failure of Islam to modernize is one of the disgraces of civilization. I concur.

B.   I downloaded to my Kindle the book <u>The Religious Virus</u> by Craig A. James, who quotes Epicurus:

Is God willing to prevent evil, but not able? Then he is not omnipotent.

Is he able, but not willing? Then he is malevolent.

Is he both able and willing? Then whence comes evil?

Is he neither able nor willing? Then why call him God?

I have heard the palaver trying to answer such questions, and it all comes down to "faith." Faith is belief without evidence. I am not immune to this, having promised "someone" that if a close relative recovered from illness, I would never quit the choir. The relative recovered (A miracle?), and I have stayed in the Choir for 17 years singing to what I believe is a rather cult-like view of Jesus as superhero.

I ask myself why, since Jesus' teachings are so profoundly right to me when it comes to behavior, do we have to objectify a "personal savior" who sits around worrying about me all the time? Why tell our children fables and silliness about Jesus' doing supernatural things, awakening the dead, changing water into wine, calming seas, and multiplying fish?

Why cannot we focus on his teachings and not his party tricks? This comes from a fellow who got his older cousin to admit to him, when he was five, that Santa was not real. (And she got in trouble for doing so!). The Sunday School Jesus is no more real than Santa, but his teachings are very real, better than Santa's actually.

C.   The closest I came to answering the question, "Why do religious teachers and devotees claim to believe in the supernatural?" comes from introductory words to

"The Life of Buddha and Its Lessons" by Henry Steel Olcutt, 1912, free on Kindle from Amazon.

He says:

The thoughtful student, in scanning the religious history of the race, has one fact continually forced upon his notice, viz., that there is an invariable tendency to deify whomsoever shows himself superior to the weakness of our common humanity. Look where we will, we find the saint-like man exalted into a divine persona and worshiped for a god. Though perhaps misunderstood, reviled, and even persecuted while living, the apotheosis (deification) is almost sure to come after death, and the victim of yesterday's mob, raised to the state of an intercessor in heaven, is besought with prayer and tears, and placatory penances, to mediate with God for the pardon of human sin.

He calls this a "mean, vile, trait of human nature," and I agree with him. How can one NOT want to defeat or conquer a neighboring country or religion if it does not recognize your "special savior"?! It is much harder to justify killing someone because his views or preferences are different from mine (Oliver Wendell Holmes Jr.'s "can't helps") than if the views derive from divine or natural law. By deifying such people, we gain a certitude that justifies wars, crusades, and jihads. Think only of the fellow in Norway who killed 90 people, mostly children, because Europe allows too many Muslims into their countries. So, also, Hitler used his "religion" to justify the Holocaust.

In dealing with people in my practice for nearly 40 years, among those who cause the hair on the back of my head to prickle are the loudly self-professed Christians. And, one of the crookedest I have dealt with so far was the Egyptian Muslim man who sold us our home property and his Virginia lawyer. I had to deal with him through three intermediaries, and at every single critical stage, he was busy praying toward Mecca. When we met face to face and shook hands, the problems ended, so maybe I do him an injustice and should blame the intermediaries. I think he used the intermediaries to wear me out and gain an advantage. I am sure he deals with "unbelievers" differently than with believers.

So, in spite of the wonderful good that religion sometimes accomplishes, at its core, it wants to do the thinking for us. It wants to tell us what we must believe, and it wants to convert us and make us believe as it teaches.

In reading about Buddha, I learned he was a rich man who learned poverty, and became the most devout of the monks. They revered him and his teaching, but, his devoted followers fell into the same trap as Islam and Christianity after a few generations. In order to make their guy better than our guy, they invented a full panoply of supernatural miracles and accomplishments. Things he had never believed about himself.

I thank my friend Larry for turning me to a couple of books on secular Buddhism. I love the idea of a spiritual quest, but in the end, even secular Buddhism wants to set down the rules. I want to figure out the rules for myself. So, I will be in choir singing, if they still let me, and the tear will still come to the eye and the catch in the throat, but I won't be in Sunday school. Can you imagine my spouting that stuff there? I have been assured that would not be the case. But I will not go to Sunday School and attempt to "convert" my classmates to my way of thinking.

And, lest you want to call me an atheist, I have NO IDEA WHAT IS OUT THERE, one minute before the big bang, one mile OUTSIDE the universe. The Spaghetti Monster is as good a guess as anything. I tend to see a "Matrix"- like, god-like, Gamer with a sense of humor, programing our bizarre world. I have taken two college level courses on cd's on The Origins of Life, and Biology, the Science of Life, and this stuff is so complex, I can barely understand the questions, let alone the answers. And I will not accept the label "agnostic." I may change my mind about this stuff tomorrow.

But, I will tell you a secret: for the politicians who claim, for whatever reason, they do not believe in

evolution, there is NO such doubt among scientists. Evolution is established to a scientific certainty! So, are the politicians dumb, or cynical, or just pandering? I suggest a combination, depending on the politician. I know Mitt Romney is backing out of the teachings of John Smith of where the Garden of Eden was. But, Michelle Bachman and Rick Perry may believe this stuff, even to the point where they want Christians to have dominion over the world by holding all the key power positions. That is scary.

Why do I post these views here? Because shallow views on religion and radical views on politics, espoused on FB, tend to wear me out. So, I will set out my position once and shut up. If 2-3 of you read this, great! I am sorry to offend anyone.

But, to me, giving God credit for some one's being lucky enough to be saved in a plane crash, yet giving him a "free ride" for killing all the rest of the passengers, JUST MAKES NO SENSE. Why can't we realize that even the most brilliant person on earth isn't sure of these things? The atheists have their valid points, but their arrogance sort of ruins it. And, their efforts to stamp out every sign of our Judeo-Christian tradition and history makes them a hated group.

After all, even our founding fathers gave lip service to "The Almighty." I say, "live and let live," but stop teaching the supernatural to our children. I am happy to admit I don't know the ultimate answers, but I work a lot harder to figure them out than you might think. I think everyone should be curious of why we are here and what we are about. My wife Nancy and I were listening to the ocean last night as I edited my blog to become a Kindle book. We heard the constant noise of the waves and watched its ebb and flow and it occurred to me, if we truly understood that one thing, we would have a clue to what it is all about.

9. Anthony Bourdain, Suicide, and The Meaning of It All

I said to a good Facebook friend, "Thanks for getting an interesting discussion going on FB about this man's tragic suicide. I am not competing, but I would like to address the question raised by the talking heads, who are going through all the predictable motions, with predictable negligible impact."; and, "Why are suicides on the increase? Since I am holding on to my own small part of this huge elephant (My family law practice has been touched by @ a dozen fatalities, 2/3's of which were suicides), I share this draft of my next blog article for your input and consideration."

A.   My reading leads me to believe that as humankind's mental capabilities evolved and increased, and as our awareness of the dangers all around, and the inevitability of our deaths, became apparent, we perfected something the other animals simply do not have; "WORRY".

B.   Most animals evidence fear, as you can see when the deer or bunny bounds away, or the Mourning Dove bursts into the air with its frightened call, but look at them two minutes later, heads down, eating peacefully, but alert to future dangers. They don't obsess or worry. I doubt they are even aware they are going to die.

C.   Then picture the apes in Kubrick's and Clarke's classic, "2001 a Space Odyssey", just before dawn the day they discovered the monolith. They are huddled together, cringing in fear from sounds of Saber Tooth Tigers and other predators. But they aren't yet "special", and they aren't thriving. In Arthur C. Clarke's vision, they are a marginal species, just hanging on.

D.   If Clarke's imagination was fact, however, those critters would not be worriers, yet; and I'll bet that in spite of the hardship, suicide was nearly zero.

E.   But then that monolith shows up, patterns our brains to make tools, and that forerunner of the military style rifle and nuclear bomb, a thigh bone with a knobby end (whack!). But once our brains get that large and creative, worry arrives, including worry about "the hereafter".

F.   How did our predecessors deal with all that worry, especially fear of dying? And, in spite of that worry, suicides were rare for hundreds of thousand years. What happened?

G.   Look at the caves of France, Chauvet and Lascaux, and the pregnant woman effigy doll found in what is now Germany, from 30,000 to 40,000 years ago. By then, we had begun to visualize and imagine, to worry, to

279

philosophize and hypothesize, and to make tools and appreciate "things".

H.   Inevitably, some of the smarter critters, for reasons I try to imagine, but at least partly to control and organize the rest, came up with a solution.

I.   The better ones may also have wanted to provide comfort and peace, but, remember, empathy and compassion weren't well-developed. Egyptian "priests" were not generally devout or compassionate. Things were getting complicated, and solutions were contemplated. But we had no scientists and no concept of the scientific method. Their math, while miraculous for the day, lasted essentially unchanged for 3000 years. It sure was not calculus!

J.   Those challenges somehow brought forth the great religious teachers and philosophers, including but by no means exclusively, the teachings of someone we call "Jesus of Nazareth", "The Christ". Collaborative creatures eventually discovered compassion and empathy, but first we just needed to get organized. We still had to fight to survive, and suicide remained rare.

K.   The early "witch doctors", shamans, medicine men, priests, prophets, and philosophers, most of whom, unfortunately, were patriarchal men, knew nothing of science. And they did not understand the fundamental principles of existence, time, matter, motion, space, DNA, evolution, or life.

L.   They knew what they could see, that sometimes pigs hosted intestinal parasites, some plants were poisonous, as were some animals, and that occasionally people acted wacko. They saw these people as possessed by demons to be exorcised. They experienced terrible storms, floods that became legend, volcanic eruptions, shooting stars, comets, and eclipses. And, they had no clue what caused them. They personified them and desired to placate the entities that caused them.

M. So, they made up stuff. If we look at it objectively now, we see they had no pipeline to any GOD; no hint they had been visited by intelligent aliens, no ancient cell phones or motorbikes; "Nada"! But, they thought hard and deep, sometimes consumed hallucinogens, and sometimes acted with cynical fraud, and claimed brilliant, supernatural insights.

N. It followed that they needed miracles and interventions by gods and spirits. So they invented them, and peopled "believed" and "had faith". But not objective fact or evidence.

O. And they provided certainty: "Follow 'our rules' and you will be just fine."

P. "Rely on someone else to do the thinking. Fail to do so, and you will be punished!"

Q. Where faith wavered or behavior deteriorated, we had good old animal and human sacrifice, and, later, threats of fire and brimstone, everlasting torture, unless we "toed the line".

R. I won't list a bunch of names here, but many of my Facebook friends are thinking deeply on these subjects. That's why I can interact with friends in Ca., Fla.,

Michigan, Israel, Tasmania, and Libya, because I find people who are wondering about these same things.

S.   No one puts more mental energy on the challenges to modern religion than my dear friend Joe JB Shaver. Try getting through your FB day, if you are his friend, without hearing from Bishop Spong, Steve McSwain, or The Dalai Lama. J.B. keeps you tuned in. "Welcome God 5.3.", he cheerfully says each day.

T.   Then there are the "new atheists", Dawkins, Evans, Hitchens, Anderson, and Jacoby. (the latter two probably shouldn't be lumped with the three former, but all are "secularists".)

U.   If you take away the myths, strip religion of the supernatural, tell the truth based on the evidence, and don't replace it with anything, life can be truly terrifying. When we die, it is simply over except for the memories that live in others. That seems natural to me, but it scares most of us, and me once in a while.

V.   If there is no "natural law" underlying our values, what are our values? If we won't burn in hell, why do we do good? Why not be in the local drug cartel or Taliban or Isis cell? They'll look out for you and help you prey on others.

W.   That's what I struggle with when I suggest we abandon the myths, the impossible stories, the threats, the moral elitism and the, "We'll do the thinking for you." attitude of most religions. What do we replace them with? I suggest reason, compassion, empathy, curiosity, and passion. And here's why.

X.	I fall back on Supreme Court Justice Oliver Wendell Holmes III's essay, "Natural Law". He talks about our desire for the superlative, our belief, especially our certitude when drunk says, "It is not enough for the knight of romance that you agree that his lady is a very nice girl—if you do not admit that she is the best that God ever made or will make, you must fight."

Y.	I rely on what I learned from him while in law school, have paid attention, to parents, grandparents, teachers, coaches, and mentors. I have watched other lawyers, especially the brilliant and impassioned ones that come in from all over the country to speak at our WVAJ events. And, I've been attracted to the "good guys" and "good girls". They're the ones who I want to be my friends.

Z.	In Sunday School, Methodist Youth Fellowship, Cub Scouts, The YMCA, choir, chorus, school, college, and everything else I did, I noticed those people and wanted to emulate them. 4-H had "Charting". The manual's title was in Greek, Gnothi seauton., "know thyself".

AA.	I weighed the evidence, and then I wrapped my arms around my own "can't helps" as Holmes called them; values and qualities that a whole human being should have. Then I worked as hard as this flawed human being could, failing miserably at times, to "be a good boy" as I promised my Mother I would be. A Good Boy is what she drilled into my head. Mine may be no better than yours, but I "feel" that they are right.

BB.	I think it has been a blessing to have been obsessed with this subject since my earliest memories. But I am struggling with the best way to help the person who just wants to live a happy, fulfilled, life. If they are going to "dead, dead and gone" as the old '60's song "And When I Die" https://youtu.be/SFEewD4EVwU , then what's it all about? Why should we care? And why the hell are things changing so fast?

CC.   These questions scare the shit out of people, so they turn to drugs, alcohol, movements, meditation, and "strong leaders" and "inspirational leaders" for answers. In an age of "accelerating change" the problem of suicide it increasing. For now that is my working hypotheses. Our country is too consumer based. We brilliant apes are not adapting fast enough. We cannot process the dangers, our food, environment, drugs, information, and misinformation. The resultant stress is enormous.

DD.   I intend to keep studying, to come up with my own solutions, and not to let someone else do the thinking.

EE.   Dawkins and Evans, the atheists, fall one step short, I believe, of my lame answer. They just detest religion. They do not provide a viable alternative to the average person, then non-scholar.

FF.   My friend J.B. wants religion to adapt and change. Bishop Spong likes to talk "gobbledygook" so the people who need old-time religion will sign on to his "new way". It's not that I disagree with him. He really is urging people to reject myth, tribalism, and judgmental thinking.   It's just that he seems to be making the same choice the old myth makers did, "Follow me, and I will lead you to the light."

GG. Maybe that's what I am doing, but I just want people to think critically, to read and watch things of quality, to wake up each day with passion and commitment, and to seek truth, regardless of your "faith" or "wish". Don't buy a "pig in a poke"; do not believe something because it is in the Bible or the priest or pastor tells you to.

HH. Do your homework and seek truth.

For now, I will just have to admit, I do not know. I am still trying to figure it out.

VIII.
FINAL THOUGHTS

I largely suspended my blogging this summer. I will return with zest this fall. I hope that 75% of this book has "green content", meaning something that will have relevance for 5 or more years. Much of my "how to" stuff should remain relevant, and the tech stuff should at least point you in the directions of the problems that must be solved. I will continue to work on figuring my place in the world, our past, present, and future. I can't get enough of that.

The new child custody law that I reference will change WV family law, perhaps profoundly. I will write of my experiences, but even now the tradition of a young child needing to stay primarily with Mother seems to be drifting away. I hope the men are up to it and will not simply hand the baby over to Grandma and girlfriend.

So, too, the concept that the primary custodian, often the Mother, can move with the child to another state with a new husband or for a new job is becoming a "crap shoot". I predict that most will not be permitted to take the child with them.

The attack by big business, insurance, and politics on our civil justice system will continue as will the attempts to marginalize "the little guy". Consumer advocates and those of a liberal bent will be savaged by the real "fake news", and I will remain a stubborn political "militant moderate".

This book goes to print at a time where the leader of our country has no regard for truth, ethics, or morality. In fact, his "regard" is for the exact opposite. And his hatred is spreading.

As I write these "final thoughts", two of our five WV Supreme Court Justices have resigned. One has retired and been indicted. The two remaining are facing impeachment. One is likely to go to prison for a long while. I predict they all will be driven from office, and their replacements appointed by the Governor.

My efforts to have a significant impact on my profession, serving on the WV Association for Justice Board of Governors, the WV State Bar Board of Governors, and teaching a variety of CLE seminars, have largely failed. Civility is not the norm in family law, nor are mediation, unbundling of legal services, or taking on accelerating change with zest and courage becoming the norm.

WV Citizens have never been this dispirited, but islands of optimism and courage remain, and the beauty remains in every county of our emerald State.

I have no plans to retire, but, as I have written, my focus will be on my clients, my family, and my friends. Time passes quickly, and one must savor each moment with passion and not just "go through the motions".

Even with all these pessimistic comments, I remain an optimist and think we will lurch forward and back, but with a net forward movement, and eventually become something no one can now predict.

I hope my readers learn some things of value. Thanks for giving it a try.

Burton Hunter

ABOUT THE AUTHOR

The values I bring to my law practice - hard work, client service and giving back to the community – are old-fashioned, but not outmoded. They come from my experience with youth fellowship at Christ United Methodist Church when I was growing up here in West Virginia. They come from Cub Scouts and 4-H, and from our excellent public school system. Later, my values were shaped by the Linsly Military Institute, where I attended 8th - 12th grades.

I graduated from West Virginia Wesleyan College in Buckhannon with a B.A. in government and history. I received my law degree from the West Virginia University College of Law. After law school, I served four years in the U.S. Air Force Jag Corps, where I earned the Air Force Commendation Medal.

After attending the Skip Barber Racing School in Connecticut, I raced for two seasons with the Sports Car Club of America, finishing second in my class the second year. I've got the competitive and strategic nature required for success in both auto racing and the practice of law.

During the 1990s, I was the recipient of the West Virginia Trial Lawyer Association's (now West Virginia Association of Justice) Member of the Year and President's awards. I have also served as president of the Upshur County Bar Association.

A Life of Learning and Service: I come from a family whose members tend to work beyond regular retirement age. So far, I "feel" young and vigorous and plan to follow their lead. Each year, I try to attend several times the hours of continuing legal education required by the West Virginia State Bar. I get a kick out of lawyers scrambling at the last minute to complete their requirements or attending a seminar in an area of law they do not even practice just because it was connected to a West Virginia University football game. I have never stopped learning and never intend to.

In my hometown of Buckhannon, I coached youth soccer for 17 years. I have also served as president of the Upshur County Senior Center, chaired the United Way campaign and sat on the board of the Upshur County Family Resources Center. I was a member of the Buckhannon Rotary Club and the Buckhannon-Upshur Chamber of Commerce. I enjoy singing in the Chapel Hill United Methodist Church choir.

When I'm not working or involved in community activities, I enjoy flat water kayaking on the Cheat River. I'm making a return trip to the Skip Barber Racing School. And I've taken up Irish Road Bowling. I'm a founding father of the West Virginia Irish Road Bowling Association, Inc.

I met my wife, Nancy Goodfellow, at West Virginia Wesleyan College, and we were married in 1969. We have four wonderful, accomplished, children, John, Christopher, Justin, and Laura, three beautiful daughters-in-law, and six precious grandchildren.

ACKNOWLEDGEMENTS

To my staff, family and mentors, my sincere thanks for your help in this endeavor.

Made in the USA
Middletown, DE
13 December 2019